The MONOCLE
Travel Guide Series

5 Ⓜ

Madrid

For more information,
please visit *gestalten.com*

Bibliographic information
published by the Deutsche
Nationalbibliothek: The Deutsche
Nationalbibliothek lists this publication in the Deutsche National-
bibliografie; detailed bibliographic
data are available online
at *dnb.d-nb.de*

Monocle editor in chief:
Tyler Brûlé
Monocle editor: *Andrew Tuck*
Series editor: *Joe Pickard*
Guide editor: *Liam Aldous*

Designed by *Monocle*
Proofreading by *Monocle*
Typeset in *Plantin & Helvetica*

Printed by *Offsetdruckerei
Grammlich, Pliezhausen*

Made in Germany

Published by *Gestalten*, Berlin 2015
ISBN 978-3-89955-624-7

2nd printing, 2016

Welcome
—— Revel in a city reawakened

Madrid is a changed city. Even as the worst of the economic crisis hit, we sat and watched with admiration as the *Spanish capital* took matters into its own hands, fuelling a metamorphosis that has transformed it for the better.

Unlike other Spanish destinations, Madrid hasn't bowed to the tourist hordes in order to weather the economic downturn. Instead, the regeneration has been led by *Madrileños* themselves. Today tradition and modernity thrive side by side, so you can marvel at the *centuries-old masterpieces* inside the Prado Museum one moment and enjoy sumptuous morsels cooked up by a new generation of *modern, intrepid chefs* the next.

Sure the landlocked city lacks a sandy beach but this also means its collective energy is poured into *nocturnal frolics* in the endless mix of *restaurants*, *bars* and *clubs*. In fact the native penchant for a good time is such an irrefutable character trait that we challenge you not to be affected by Madrid's contagiously cheerful spirit.

Gone are the days of the stuffy Spanish capital that outlying regions once scoffed at as too provincial. After decades of immigration from around the country, and plenty of *international flavour* too, the city has thrown off the shackles of immovable tradition. What was once a buttoned-down bastion of conservatism has become Spain's unabashed centre of *the avant-garde*.

This newly reinvented Madrid is a melting pot of talent, taste and citywide tenacity, all courtesy of a population of fun-loving, *welcoming residents*. — (M)

Contents
—— Navigating the city

Use the key below to help navigate the guide section by section.

 Hotels

 Food and drink

 Retail

 Things we'd buy

Essays

Culture

Design and architecture

Sport and fitness

Walks

Madrid's transformation from crusty conformity to artistic adventurism is in full swing. Whether you're in the market for world-beating museums or avant-garde galleries – or just want to unwind with a drink at an intimate music venue – our pick of the city's cultural offerings will have something to suit your mood.

There's always plenty going on in Madrid and no wonder: this is one of Europe's most densely populated cities. Luckily, that means eye-catching architecture everywhere you look, from great public projects to modest, old-world backstreets and plazas.

There's no need to put your fitness regime on hold while on holiday. We've rounded up the best places to get physical, and put together a few cycling and running routes to help you make the most of Madrid's green spaces. Plus: the finest grooming emporiums to keep you looking your very best.

There is no better way to understand the nuances of Madrid than setting off into its network of narrow streets. Our five themed walks take you through our favourite neighbourhoods, breaking off every now and then for curio-crammed shops and appealing, home-cooked bites.

Be in the know with our bite-size guide to events, slang and the city's soundtrack. Plus tips on what to do on a rainy day.

Find out more about our global brand, from groundbreaking print, radio, online and film output through to our cafés and shops.

The people who put this guide together: writers, photographers, researchers and all the rest.

Map
—— The city at a glance

Opinions about where Madrid's *barrios* begin and end are about as diverse as the districts themselves. It's not just the tangled nature of the city's streets that blur the lines of demarcation but also the fact that districts have evolved and splintered since the first maps were drawn up.

Modern Madrid now has a clearer, more localised sense of neighbourhood identity so what many decades ago was referred to as Universidad is now divided into Malasaña and Conde Duque. A rebranding of Huertas into Barrio de Las Letras in 2005 was intended to honour the district's literary past (although the name is yet to be universally accepted). Meanwhile it's nearly impossible to know where El Rastro fits into the narrow, winding streets of La Latina (so we've put them together).

With the help of our map we hope you'll find yourself as informed and up to date with Madrid's varied (albeit often hard to differentiate) *barrios* as the capital's residents.

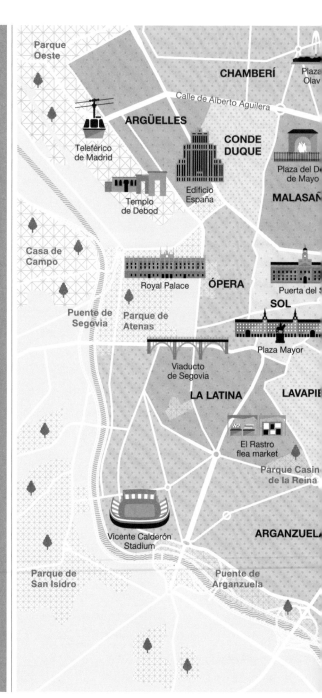

Plaza de Toros de
Las Ventas

Parque Eva
Duarte

SALAMANCA

MADRID-BARAJAS
AIRPORT

mercado de la paz

Quinta de la
Fuente del Berro

**LAS
SALESAS**

Plaza de
Colón

Mercado de
la Paz

Calle de O'Donnell

HUECA

Puerta de
Alcalá

Palacio de Cibeles
RTES (Madrid City Hall)
& CentroCentro

Parque del
Buen Retiro

Parque
de Roma

LAS
ETRAS

Museo Nacional
del Prado

Palacio de Cristal

RETIRO

Calle del Dr Esquerdo

Autopista de Circunvalación M30

Fountain of
the Fallen Angel

REINA

SOFIA

Museo Nacional
Centro de
Arte Reina Sofía

Atocha
Railway Station

Museo del Ferrocarril
de Madrid
(Railway Museum)

Matadero Madrid

**Parque Enrique
Tierno Galván**

0   500m

N

Need to know
—— Get to grips with the basics

How to order cold draft beer, what areas in Madrid to avoid and some history tips – the following pages will come in handy during your visit to the Spanish capital. Remember, *Madrileños* are approachable and ready to help – so ask if you need directions or assistance with selecting your tapas.

Feast or famine
Opening hours

The Spanish timetable takes some getting used to. In a city this nocturnal, you're just going to have to accept that the clock ticks to a different beat. Most mornings cafés won't open until 10.00, lunch is served between 14.00 and 16.00 and you'll have to wait until about 21.00 for a good dinner. While we think it's best to go with the *Madrileño* flow, sometimes those gnawing hunger pangs are a little too much to bear. Fortunately a growing number of places are keeping their kitchens open all day (look for the *horario continuo* on the menu), or you can duck into one of the sprawling gastronomic markets for an uninterrupted feast.

Heart of the city
Districts

Puerta del Sol is not only the centre of Madrid but also of Spain. All of the major highway distances are measured from the "Kilometre zero" point. The spot is marked by a plaque on the pavement outside the 18th-century red-brick Casa de Correos. Unfortunately, over the years, the three-block radius around the city's "Gate of the Sun" has been overrun by tourist-focused businesses and many of the streets and plazas in this nucleus have fallen into disrepair. So be advised: Madrid's real beauty revolves around the central Sol district but rarely within it. Walk a few minutes in any direction from the city's epicentre to get a real taste for its diverse and authentically flavoured *barrios*.

Naturally I'm the muse for Madrid's new coat of arms

Pace yourself
Dining

Food culture is everywhere you look but brushing up on the basics can help steer you through the potential mealtime maelstrom. Don't baulk at the set menus. Known as the *menú-diario*, the three-course option (with beverage option to boot) is one that *Madrileños* swear by and it is most popular at lunchtime. The only trouble may be getting the daily menu in English. You should know what tapas are but in Madrid, *raciones* are king. These bigger portions of food are meant for sharing between two and three people – so order accordingly. Beer drinkers should avoid asking for a pint; drink at a more measured pace by ordering a small *caña* instead. The landlocked city also has Spain's biggest fresh seafood market, which is a boon for restaurants. Even the city's main food icon is seaborne: the surprisingly delicious crispy-squid sandwich.

Watch your step
Walking

The constant menace of *pivotes*, Madrid's ubiquitous stunted poles, awaits on nearly every street. The chance of smashing your shin into one is painfully high. These vehicle-blocking bollards are relics of a more anarchic time when parking inspectors weren't around to rein in the chaos. Their purpose today seems mainly to punish daydreaming pedestrians, so most *Madrileños* have developed a sixth sense of supreme spatial awareness to avoid any injury. However, yours won't kick into gear until you suffer at least one excruciating crash to the knee. Sorry.

English lessons
Communication

English proficiency is improving but a significant language barrier endures. Generations of Spaniards have grown up with TV and films dubbed into Spanish, and a focus on French as a second language. However, in the past decade there has been a seismic shift: most public schools now teach half their classes in English, more people travel abroad and several inner-city "original-version" cinemas are booming. Nonetheless, residents still tend to shy away from flexing their English skills in front of colleagues for fear of ridicule. Be persistent and friendly, and emphasise "*No hablo Español*"; they often know more English than they let on. Which brings us to our next tip.

Such elegance, such poise. Your dancing is good too

Talking to strangers
Etiquette

Even if you don't speak a word of Spanish, you'll soon realise that this is a city that likes to talk – a lot. Greeting people in lifts, yelling across the street, the high decibel levels found in bars, restaurants and plazas: conversation is fluid, fast and usually loud. On packed trains, instead of saying "Excuse me," *Madrileños* even ask a question to promote further dialogue: "*Vas a salir?*" ("Are you getting off?"). The language barrier may be an issue but in the social arena people display few qualms about speaking to strangers. Don't hold back: talk to the person standing next to you at the bar and you never know where the night will end up. For more vocabulary tips see Resources on page 138.

Clues to the past
Sightseeing

Spanish history is fascinatingly full of tumult but the country still seems uncomfortable grappling with its past. History buffs take note: in Madrid there are no dedicated museums documenting the Civil War, the Spanish Inquisition or the Franco dictatorship. However, plenty of clues to these darker periods are peppered around the metropolis. Occasionally a small, inconspicuous sign is the only giveaway: the site of the Inquisition's first trial is commemorated by a plate-sized plaque near the Spanish Senate. The grandiloquent architecture of the 1950s to 1970s is a reminder of the fascist dictatorship, while the most insightful tour of

the Civil War can be found through art: namely the Reina Sofia Museum's extensive exhibition of propaganda. Madrid certainly doesn't unpack the past like Berlin but if you do your research and look hard enough, you'll make some intriguing discoveries.

Don't miss out
When to visit

In August, the landlocked capital experiences a mass exodus, as companies shut down for the entire month and workers head to the coast for a month-long break. Many discerning *Madrileños* flock to Spain's southwestern coast, which boasts sandy beaches, pine forests and fishing ports whose restaurants serve up some of Europe's finest seafood. As a result of everyone taking their break at the same time, the quietest period in Madrid is between mid-July and the end of August. With so many shutters rolled down (and handwritten notes sticky-taped to them declaring: "Gone on holidays"), a walk around the city centre can be an eerily desolate experience. If you're looking for more of a city buzz, Madrid is most alive during May, June and September. The busiest tourist season – from September to November – bucks the standard high-season trend so book those hotel rooms early.

I might finish all the crispy squid before you get here

Hotels
—— Rooms with a view

If there is one thing to take from this guide it's that Madrid isn't lacking in colour and diversity – and that's certainly the case for accommodation and hospitality. Even though quite a few hotels belong to international chains, they still have a palpable Spanish flavour to them: bespoke furnishings are made by local designers and delicious menus prepared by Madrid's top chefs. The generous patios and endless rooftop terraces offering mind-blowing views of the capital don't hurt either.

Meanwhile, many independent hotels and smaller chains have made serious investments in art displays. If you find yourself thinking that the bright hues and lavish decorations in your chosen lodging are a touch overpowering, remember: this is Madrid. Extravagance is a given.

①
Hotel de Las Letras, Cortes
Updated elegance

The eloquent Hotel de Las Letras is within walking distance of a cluster of museums and galleries. The heritage-listed, peach-coloured building was designed by architect Cesáreo Iradier in 1917 and renovated in 2005. Ornate flourishes such as the carved wooden staircase coalesce with the hotel's modern, minimalist decor. While the dense colour blocking in the 109 rooms can be a little overwhelming, the floor-to-ceiling windows filter in the Madrid sunshine and provide a prime vantage point for observing the bustle of Gran Vía.

The relaxed menu by chef Paco Morales is best enjoyed on the buzzy, plant-strewn rooftop terrace, a popular spot for sunset drinks during the warmer months.
Gran Vía 11, 28013
+34 915 237 980
hoteldelasletras.com

MONOCLE COMMENT: For the health-conscious, the hotel has a 24-hour gym with the latest stretch-and-tone equipment. Or, if the weather permits, head due east along Calle Alcalá, where you'll find the city's outdoor sporting facilities in the Buen Retiro Park (see page 110).

②
Room Mate Alicia, Las Letras
Winning form

Former Olympic equestrian Kike Sarasola founded his design-led boutique-hotel collection Room Mate in 2004. Since then the brand has become a favourite of creative types attracted to its individuality and welcoming staff.

Alicia, positioned on the bustling Plaza de Santa Ana, is one of four Room Mate locations in Madrid. Its 34 rooms are simply furnished and overlook the lively square below. The substantial daily breakfast is served in the dining room until noon, so there's no excuse for missing it.
Calle Prado 2, 28014
+34 913 896 095
alicia.room-matehotels.com

MONOCLE COMMENT: This affordable luxury alternative takes customer service seriously. Nothing is too difficult to organise, including transfers by private car, travel reservations, medical care and babysitting options.

Light meal
—
Breakfast is served in The Conservatory until 11.00

(3)
Urso, Las Salesas
Starring role

Top-notch service, an underground spa and an innovative restaurant starring new guest chefs each month are a few of the features that set Urso apart from its peers in the capital. It is also the first five-star boutique hotel in the city and makes a point of sourcing all of its food, flowers and chocolates from suppliers in the area.

Architect Antonio Obrador has conserved many of the original late-19th-century building's features, such as the tiles on the walls, the mahogany lift and the stained-glass windows in the lobby. All 78 rooms and suites profit from big windows, linen of the highest quality and custom-made furniture, while the spa offers all manner of treatments by Spanish skincare specialist Natura Bissé.
Calle Mejia Lequerica 8, 28004
+34 914 444 458
hotelurso.com

MONOCLE COMMENT: Urso's restaurant welcomes a different top chef with a special pop-up menu (and kitchen) each and every month. Everything changes, from the palate-pleasing cuisine to the palette that is used for the interior design.

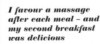
I favour a massage after each meal – and my second breakfast was delicious

Rarefied rooms

01 Urso Terrace Suite: Urso has two penthouse-style spaces, each with a separate lounge, bedroom and marble bathroom; the attached private terraces are furnished with loungers and a dining area. Sunbathe while enjoying the view or have friends over for dinner under the Spanish sky.
hotelurso.com

02 Vincci Skylight: Located on the 11th and 12th floors of Vincci Via 66, the Skylight room has its own lift and overlooks Gran Vía. It's set behind the huge, neon Schweppes sign, which has been around since 1969. The ad appeared in the film *El Día de la Bestia* and, together with Tio Pepe (*see page 120*), is one of the city's best-loved advertising landmarks. But don't worry about the neon glow: Vincci has installed special curtains to black out any glimmer of light.
vinccihoteles.com

03 The Real Suite at Villa Magna: Spread over a huge space on the top floor of the nine-storey Villa Magna, the Real offers two private en-suite bedrooms, its own steam room and office space. Great if you're travelling with your extended family; even better if you're planning a dinner party in the dining room – which is adorned with a grand piano and can easily accommodate 10 people – or on the huge terrace. Guests also enjoy private butler service. If the Real is booked, try its sibling Royal Suite. It's still big enough to house its own Japanese garden.
villamagna.es

Hospes Madrid, Salamanca
Glamour on the quiet

One of nine Hospes locations across Spain, this red-brick hotel has garnered a stellar reputation in one of the capital's most upmarket neighbourhoods. The traditional exteriors, characteristic of Madrid's architecture, sit façade to façade with the Puerta de Alcalá, which acts as the gateway to the Plaza de la Independencia. Towering ceilings and marbled trimmings offer serene relief from the bustle found beyond the grand entrance.

All of the expectations of a five-star establishment are comfortably met, making the hotel a favourite among business types and travellers chasing that delicate balance of glamour combined with a good night's sleep. Don't miss the chance to dine at the award-winning Independencia Restaurant, which is heralded for serving some of the most lauded seafood in Madrid.
*Plaza de la Independencia 3, 28001
+ 34 914 322 911
hospes.com*

MONOCLE COMMENT: The best seats in the house are to be found inside the hotel's deluxe suites. Each is afforded a grand, sweeping view over the Alcalá Gate and neighbouring Retiro Park.

Looking good
───

The Hospes Madrid recently became a Design Hotels member. The boutique hotel owes its membership to its handsome Bourbon Restoration period architecture, tranquil ambience and the Bodyna Spa that is housed in the former stables.

⑤

ME Madrid Reina Victoria,
Las Letras
Sleek and central

Founded in 1923, the Gran Hotel
Reina Victoria was once the
preferred stopover of bullfighters
and cultural heavyweights such
as Ernest Hemingway. Today
this gem in the heart of town is
known as the ME Madrid Reina
Victoria, courtesy of Meliá Hotels
International. Its historic façade
stands unchanged but the 180
rooms and 12 bespoke suites have
undergone a modern remodelling
by United Designers.

Busy jet-setters will benefit
from the 24/7 business centre
while gourmets can enjoy tapas
in Perico Cortés and Tomás
Tarruella's in-house Ana La
Santa restaurant. The rooftop bar
– known, helpfully, as The Roof
– offers spectacular views over
Plaza de Santa Ana, as well as the
many ornate spires and bustling
alleys of the capital.
Plaza de Santa Ana 14, 28012
+ 34 917 016 000
melia.com

MONOCLE COMMENT: Are you
travelling with a furry companion?
The Reina Victoria's special pet
package ensures that your sidekick
will be well taken care of during his
or her stay.

⑥

Hotel One Shot 23, Las Letras
Little gem

This second location by Hotel
One Shot, on Calle del Prado,
nestles on a strip that was once
home to antique dealers. It's in
the beating heart of the city's art
quarter and the hotel embraces the
vibrant cultural scene by garnishing
its walls with a rotating selection of
works from neighbourhood
photographers, refreshing the
images every three months or so.

Although small in stature – it
has just 42 rooms across four floors
– accommodation is spacious, with
a studio layout featuring wooden
floors that lend a home-from-home
feel to the place.

Transfers to and from the
airport in the hotel's Volvo sedan
are easy to arrange and, although
no dining is available on site, the
ornate Ateneo restaurant is just
around the corner.
Calle del Prado 23, 28014
+ 34 914 204 001
hoteloneshotprado23.com

MONOCLE COMMENT:
To best complement the original
1915 architecture (note the column
centred in the lobby and the main
staircase), One Shot enlisted the
help of Spanish lighting company
Años Luz Iluminación.

Spread out
—
The rooms
are roomy at
Hotel One
Shot 23

⑦
The Principal, Chueca
Eclectic dreams

Housed in a palatial 1917 Spanish
Renaissance-style building, The
Principal proudly spans seven
floors overlooking the always-lively
boulevard Gran Vía. It's owned
by the team behind Hotel Único
(*see page 22*) and is home to 76
rooms and suites.

Expect old-world charisma
topped with modern furnishings
and fittings. Designer Pilar
García-Nieto and the team at
Barcelona-based studio Luzio
put together the smart interiors,
preserving the building's original
high ceilings, large windows and
impressive ironwork. "We wanted
to create a mix of styles: influences
of a classic British club, the
flamboyance and glamour of a
French palace and the modern
masculinity of a Manhattan loft,"
says García-Nieto.
*Calle Marqués de Valdeiglesias 1,
28004
+ 34 915 218 743
theprincipalmadridhotel.com*

MONOCLE COMMENT: It's all about
the rooftop terraces in Madrid and
the one at The Principal is a firm
favourite, offering panoramic –
not to mention dramatic – views
over the capital.

*Straight to the
Manzanares, por
favor; I fancy
a doggy paddle*

Top draw
—
The rooftop terrace at The Principal is a must-visit

Matter of taste
—
The Principal has a sixth-floor restaurant, El Ático, that is open 24 hours a day for both guests and those just wanting to pop in for a little something. It's the ideal place for a business breakfast, lunch or dinner (all three if it's a busy day), or to have a refresher with friends.

021

Hotel Villa Magna, Salamanca
Old-world manners

Villa Magna is among Madrid's most exclusive hotels. Offering its old-school charm and class in the capital since 1972, the landmark reopened in 2007 after it was refurbished by Madrid-based designer Thomas Urquijo. Besides preserving the original façade, Urquijo made sure all 150 rooms were exquisitely decorated with restored antique furniture.

For your gastronomic enjoyment the Villa Magna Restaurant is the spot for lunch; in the evening, pop by the wood-panelled Magnum Bar for a pre-dinner *vermut*.
Paseo de la Castellana 22, 28046
+ 34 915 871 234
villamagna.es

MONOCLE COMMENT: The hotel offers 24-hour Les Clefs d'Or Concierge service, transport, a personal shopper, city tours, ticket services, restaurant reservations and much more – just name it.

⑧
Hotel Único, Salamanca
Lap of luxury

Home to Ramón Freixa's Michelin-starred restaurant, this intimate, luxurious hotel housed in a 19th-century building is set in the heart of well-heeled Salamanca. Único's lobby matches the hotel's surroundings with opulent decor: think marble mosaics, mirrored floors and elaborate chandeliers.

The lavishness of the atrium is balanced by the warm room interiors, which sport polished wooden floors, soft-coloured rugs and huge beds covered in lush linens, all courtesy of Spanish designers María José Cabré and Pilar García Nieto.

Único has 44 rooms, including six suites. To enjoy some peace and quiet book one of the King Courtyard or King Garden rooms overlooking the relaxed greenery of the hotel's patio. Meanwhile, the Grand Suite has its own lounge and hot tub.
Calle Claudio Coello 67, 28001
+ 34 917 810 173
unicohotelmadrid.com

MONOCLE COMMENT: Único is the first of two hotels in Madrid by Barcelona-bred Pau Guardans. The second, The Principal (*see page 20*), opened in 2015.

No time to waste
—
Sharpening his culinary prowess in his family's Barcelona restaurant, Ramón Freixa opened his eponymous venue at Hotel Único in 2009. It now has two Michelin stars but still room for just 35 diners so be sure to ask reception to book a table well in advance.

(10)

7 Islas Hotel, Malasaña
Shore thing

One of the few family-owned hotels in Madrid, 7 Islas was launched in 2002 by Mónica Salces Rosa and her two sisters. "It all began with a dream," she says. "Our grandfather Juan Rosa – a hotelier and businessman from Lanzarote – once imagined a 'home from home' for people from the Canary Islands in Madrid."

Thanks to Madrid-based design firm Kikekeller, the 79-room hotel in the lively Malasaña district benefits from fresh interiors in which Nordic furnishings by Danish modernist designer Børge Mogensen and Le Corbusier-trained Ilmari Tapiovaara shine alongside rustic details (think rough wooden tables and weathered lanterns).

And as quality of service is all that really matters to Salces Rosa, besides its own airport shuttle 7 Islas Hotel also offers bicycle rentals on the spot.
Calle Valverde 14, 28004
+ 34 915 234 688
hotelsieteislas.com

MONOCLE COMMENT: When not out and about exploring the bohemian borough, take a break in the lobby and order the hotel's signature 7 Islas gin-based cocktail.

Style council
—
Furnishings are a key element in 7 Islas

11
AC Santo Mauro, Chamberí
Noble hideaway

In the late 1800s, the Duke of
Santo Mauro created an oasis
on these quiet, leafy backstreets.
The three buildings and the
surrounding gardens that once
comprised his manor have since
been converted into the Marriott
AC Santo Mauro, a handily short
distance from Madrid's museums.

A regal air graces the French
neoclassical interiors of the 49
guest rooms, well-resourced
meeting rooms and conference
facilities. Most stunning is the
intricately ornamented space that
once housed the duke's library and
which is now home to the hotel's
restaurant La Biblioteca.

The intimacy of AC Santo
Mauro offers a serene alternative
to the city's characteristic liveliness,
perhaps faulted only by the
absence of a guest car service.
Calle Zurbano 36, 28010
+ 34 913 196 900
marriott.com

MONOCLE COMMENT: The indoor
pool and Turkish baths draw on
the indulgent history of this area,
once famed as the neighbourhood
favoured by Spanish nobility for
their city homes. Ask the concierge
to talk you through some of the
history of the nearby residences.

New-wave hostels

Finding a reasonably priced, well-designed place to stay is a challenge in a city dominated by big hotel chains. Luckily, Madrid is enjoying a surge in friendly, hotel-quality boutique hostels. And don't let the name fool you: it's *adiós* to bunk-bed dorms and *hola* to pretty and peaceful rooms.

01 The Hat, Sol: Hats off to this refurbished 19th-century mansion, right in between Sol and Latina, for its casual, airy minimalism. Light pine furnishings made near Toledo keep its 42 rooms simple and gracious but the primary praise here has to be the roof terrace, where open-air barbecues come with a sizzling view across the city's numerous red-tiled roofs.
thehatmadrid.com

02 Mad4You, Malasaña: The *corrala*, a traditional whitewashed courtyard, is at the heart of this 15th-century former home. Its colourful rooms look onto the wood-lined central patio to create a shared space and add to the feeling of an old-style community.
madhostel.com

03 Room007, Chueca: The vivid pop-art-style rooms of this lively venture are perfect to come back to after a night out in the vibrant Malasaña and Chueca districts that surround it. The areas aren't short of wining and dining options but Room007's own rooftop, with its rattan chairs and fairy lights, is a great place to start an evening with a cocktail from the bar.
room007.com

High class
—
Only You's attic has a dressing room

12

Hotel Only You, Chueca
Going the extra mile

It is nearly impossible to settle
on a defining feature of Hotel
Only You. Perhaps it's the
top-to-toe eclecticism of its
interiors by Spanish designer
Lázaro Rosa-Violán, which have
transformed the 19th-century
architecture into a homely
sequence of well-lit spaces.
Or maybe it's the unwavering
dedication of the staff to its
guests' myriad queries or offbeat
requests; rumour has it a staff
member once queued at a stadium
to purchase last-minute match
tickets for a football-loving guest.

Regardless, the first boutique
property under the Palladium
Hotel Group umbrella is perfectly
at home in its central location in
peppy Chueca. Nearby residents
are all too happy to attest to its
merits by filling the lounge on
a nightly basis.
Calle del Barquillo 21, 28004
+ 34 910 052 222
onlyyouhotels.com

MONOCLE COMMENT: Don't fret
if the effects of jet lag or the
consequences of a night spent on
the tiles have shifted your sleeping
patterns. The hotel's kitchen serves
an à la carte menu 24/7.

Food and drink
—— Dining destinations

The eating, the drinking, the being merry – is that all people in this city do? The answer, in short, is a robust yes. The Spanish capital's appetite knows no bounds, and in recent times a new generation of chefs and entrepreneurs have been busy upping Madrid's edible offering, transforming the city in the process.

The good part is that the best-tasting bites are not the exclusive domain of Michelin-starred restaurants (although there's plenty of them too) but can also be found wandering the *tabernas* of La Latina, the stalls of the mouthwatering food markets, or the family-run restaurants that keep their kitchens sizzling well into the night.

You'll also need a few grains of guidance to find the finest – and quirkiest – haunts for late-night cocktails or the beloved *vermut*. Your only impediment to this unlimited feast is the city's culinary timetable but we've provided plenty of ways to get around that too.

Restaurants
Pick of the top tables

Circo de las Tapas, Malasaña
Roll up, roll up

The only animals to be seen at Antonio de Santiago's (*pictured*) "Tapas Circus" are of the edible variety. However, the owner is an ever-accommodating ringmaster who provides his audience with plenty of Spanish charm and an enticing menu of no-nonsense dishes. The laidback Mediterranean vibe makes it an ideal stopover for a spot of lunch, and the daily menu (scribbled on the front window) adds a pinch of old-style authenticity.

Restaurant by day and thriving bar by night (though you can still book a table for dinner if you want), "el Circo" attracts a diverse crowd that reflects Madrid's open and inclusive mentality. And whatever you do, don't leave without sampling the tasty *tortilla de patatas*.
Calle Corredera Baja de San Pablo 21, 28004
+34 686 044 746
circodelastapas.com

Superior grazing
—

Head to department store El Corte Inglés' Gourmet Experience atop its Callao and Calle Serrano stores. You'll find offerings from Madrid stalwarts such as David Muñoz's StreetXO, Estanislao Carenzo's Chifa Boteco and Roberto Ruiz's Cascabel.
elcorteingles.eu

TriCiclo, Las Letras
Beyond the sea

A trio of up-and-coming chefs opened this adventurous restaurant in 2013. Friends Javier Goya, Javier Mayor (*pictured, Goya left*) and David Alfonso honed their skills in some of Spain's finest kitchens and are now in charge of their own dishes, which people are lining up to sample (reservations are an absolute necessity). The place specialises in seafood that is embellished with imaginative flavour; think Galician scallops with coconut, lime and strawberries. The three-route menu may be confusing but chart your course by ordering the half portion-sized *raciones* and share as a group.

A little way down the street, the company has opened a second restaurant called Tándem. Described as a "younger brother", it offers a more casual atmosphere with service from 10.30 until well after midnight.
Calle Santa María 28, 28014
+ 34 910 244 798
eltriciclo.es

Tapas streets

01 Calle Cava Baja, La Latina: The commotion inside the bars and *tabernas* of La Latina reaches fever pitch at the weekend but Cava Baja is the most concentrated strip of sumptuous tapas. It is home to centuries-old establishments such as Casa Lucio and plenty of other spots in which to graze the day away.

02 Calle Ponzano, Chamberí: Legend has it Calle Ponzano has more bars and restaurants than any other street in western Europe. The trouble is, there are so many that you might lose count due to the inevitable self-induced overdose. Start at the bottom, heading north, and keep your eyes peeled for the seasonally themed fresh-food window displays.

03 Calle Jesús, Las Letras: The outstretched arms of the good Lord himself welcome people to this short tract of ancient gems. Start with a glass of wine or *vermut* and some *banderillas* at the Taberna de Dolores, then work your way to the next venue, admiring the antiquity-laden walls of each haunt as you go.

Eating 'raciones' past midnight? What can I say – I'm a night owl

③
La Candelita, Chueca
Latin spirit

This sharply appointed fusion-tapas bar and restaurant wears its Latin American influences on its sleeve. From the low-level seating amid tropical artwork, revolving ceiling fans and dark wooden accents you can journey across the continent via a menu that boasts freshly prepared ceviche, delicate empanadas and hearty Colombian staple *bandeja paisa*: a substantial serving of rice, plantain, chorizo and egg.

The perfect place to share a few dishes among friends, it also offers the requisite drinks menu: think cold beers and caipirinhas.
Calle del Barquillo 30, 28004
+ 34 915 238 553
lacandelita.es

④
Ultramarinos Quintín, Salamanca
Deep-sea dining

This quaint-looking restaurant on the affluent Jorge Juan shopping strip pays homage to the former tenant: a traditional seafood merchant or *ultramarino*. The menu includes lots of fresh fish as well as a delicious dish of mussel ravioli.

Sandro Silva and Marta Seco opened their third restaurant on the heels of their two other successful ventures: Ten Con Ten and El Paraguas (which sits across the road). The vibrant interior is reminiscent of a food market and has quickly established itself as the place to be seen in the sophisticated Salamanca district.
Calle Jorge Juan 17, 28001
+ 34 917 864 624

⑤
Magasand, Salamanca
Get your fill

A short hop from the Retiro Metro station in the well-heeled district of Salamanca, sharp contemporary styling sets this sandwich joint apart. With plenty of respectable reading material to peruse it's a chic spot for a solo lunch of baguettes, pizza or soup.

Expect to see a cool young crowd amid concrete pillars and industrial seating, drawn in by the savvy magazine selection and changing art exhibits. There's also a picnic service: stock up and head to nearby Parque del Buen Retiro for lunch on the grass.
Calle Columela 4, 28001
+ 34 915 768 843
magasand.com

⑥
Kabuki Wellington, Salamanca
Nikkei hits new high

Helmed by acclaimed chef Ricardo Sanz, this Michelin-starred restaurant is one of the city's standout purveyors of *Nikkei* cuisine, which fuses Peruvian and Japanese tastes. The sleek modern dining room takes Japanese design cues, with a row of sushi chefs working intently off to one side. If it weren't for the smiling Spanish waiting staff you could almost forget you were in Madrid at all.

There are other subtle hints of the Mediterranean to be found on the menu, such as the *sashimi de toro* (bull's tail sashimi). Essentially, if you're on the hunt for mouthwatering morsels in a formal setting, Kabuki ticks all the right boxes. Just don't forget to save room for the dessert menu, designed by renowned pastry chef Oriol Balaguer.
Calle Velázquez 6, 28001
+ 34 915 777 877
restaurantekabuki.com

01 Petra Mora, Salamanca: This vibrant, home-styled delicatessen on Calle Ayala abounds in colour and choice, bringing together more than 600 of Spain's most beloved delicacies and products to give them a well-designed packaging makeover. Fill your own gift pack with an array of Spanish preserves, cold meats, cheeses and wines, as well as fading food traditions such as truffle-infused eggs and chestnut purée.
petramora.com

02 Casa Mira, Las Letras: Spaniards are absolutely nuts about nougat. Even the way they say it is eminently more fun: *turrón*. Practise rolling your R's as you wait patiently for Casa Mira's chatty, welcoming team of assistants to neatly package your selection of Spanish sweetness. Some of the items on offer are handmade truffles, *peladillas* and marzipan. It's a well-rehearsed operation: the family business dates back to 1842, when it was founded by Luis Mira.
casamira.es

03 Bodega de los Reyes, Conde Duque: Discerning husband-and-wife team Javier and Sonia run this well-stocked wine shop on a Conde Duque corner, combining more than 25 years of experience with over 4,000 vintage varietals housed across two floors. The shop runs multilingual wine tastings every Friday and Saturday, guiding you effortlessly through the nuances of each grape.
labodegadelosreyes.com

Federal Café, Conde Duque
For morning people

Madrileños have never really jumped aboard the big-breakfast bandwagon; the most elaborate indigenous rendition consisted mainly of tomato toast served with coffee the colour and consistency of crude oil. Even the word "brunch" seems to have been lost in translation. The two Australians behind Federal Café have been nudging Madrid's morning food culture toward a more Antipodean interpretation though, with flat whites, poached eggs and a host of other creative concoctions.

The pair brought their successful Barcelona café brand to Madrid in 2013 and their kitchen stays open from 09.00 to 23.00, meaning lunch and dinner are also tasty options. The relaxed atmosphere has become a beacon for freelancers in search of their requisite caffeine refuel.
Plaza Comendadoras 9, 28015
+34 915 328 424
federalcafe.es/madrid

La Cocina del Desierto, Chueca *Closed*
Souk it up

Centuries of Islamic occupation have left an indelible mark on Madrid's architecture. Morocco is one of Spain's closest neighbours but this doesn't make the hunt for an authentic Moroccan restaurant in the capital any easier. Most of them are confined to the Lavapiés district but this vibrant offering in Chueca is a worthy exception.

The souk-like cave creates a truly atmospheric space with low ceilings – and even lower lighting – a backdrop of luxuriant silks, engraved brass tables and brightly coloured *azulejo* tiling. The visual feast is stacked against the equally delicious menu, offering generous servings of *shawarma*, subtly spiced couscous dishes and satisfying portions of lamb tagine. House rules apply here, which means there's every chance you could find yourself sitting on the ground.
Calle de Barbieri 1, 28004
+34 915 231 142

9
Punto MX, Salamanca
Maximum Mexican

You'd think the strong historical and linguistic ties between Spain and Mexico would extend to the local gastronomy. But Spaniards barely eat spicy food and until recently they didn't care too much about Mexican cuisine either. Roberto Ruiz's award-winning restaurant Punto MX has been on a mission to change these misguided perceptions, earning a Michelin star in the process; it's the only Mexican restaurant in Europe to boast one.

Ruiz embraces the complexity of Mexican flavours with a spice-filled haute-cuisine menu that sizzles with surprises. The adjacent Mezcal Lab bar, helmed by expert Martin Eccius, offers the largest collection of *mezcal* in Europe, and some have been paired to particular dishes. The *mezcaliñas* are lethal but mandatory.
Calle General Pardiñas 40, 28001
+ 34 914 022 226
puntomx.es

10
Murillo Café, Retiro
In the frame

Named after one of Spain's most revered painters, Murillo Café sits on a picturesque corner behind the Prado Museum; its relaxed vibe offers the perfect post-gallery spot at which to refuel. Opened in 1927, its antler-clad exposed brick walls enclose an intimate space for an afternoon tea of freshly baked breads, pastries and magdalena cupcakes. The menu also includes salads and steaks.

Ask for a table under the dappled shade of the pavement terrace: an excellent spot for surveying the art-hungry hordes.
Calle Ruiz de Alarcón 27, 28014
+ 34 913 693 689
murillocafe.com

11
Nakeima, Argüelles
Get in line

A no-reservation policy means securing a seat here can be a challenge: flocks of early birds queue up for an hour before the street-side door opens 30 minutes before each service (13.30 for lunch and 20.30 for dinner).

The team behind Nakeima – still all in their twenties – show plenty of promise; most of them cut their teeth alongside some of Spain's best chefs (David Muñoz, the Roca brothers) and their Spanish-Japanese fusion cuisine is matched by their playful energy. The sumptuous *nigiris* and a tasty twist on Madrid's classic squid sandwich are essential.
Calle Meléndez Valdés 54, 28015

Poncelet Cheese Bar, Chamberí
Put dairy in your diary

The arresting aroma hits you as soon as you enter the wooden confines of this venue, which ventures well beyond simple cheeseboards. Evolving out of a successful retail venture, the restaurant has been pasteurised with an educational theme as its core ingredient. In the far corner a cheesemaster guides a select audience through the nuances of yellow, white and blue variations, while diners get the opportunity to feast on cheese tapas, larger dishes and degustation menus.

Upstairs a "cheese library" hosts tasting seminars and there's even an in-house publication: the "cheesepaper". An impressive vertical garden moderates the smell and if none of the 190 varieties on offer float your boat, opt for the cheese-free menu (or go somewhere that doesn't specialise in cheese).
Calle José Abascal 61, 28003
+ 34 913 992 550
ponceletcheesebar.es

(13)
Restaurante Botín, Sol
Timeless classic

Tucked away in the cavernous outer perimeter of Plaza Mayor, this family-run restaurant has been perfecting dishes such as suckling pig and roasted lamb inside its wood-fired oven for aeons – longer than anyone else, in fact.

That's because this, the world's oldest restaurant, has been serving tables since 1725. It's impolite to dwell on the topic of age though. What really matters is the food, which draws on centuries of perfected techniques and age-old gastronomic traditions. (Did we mention how old the place is?)

Calle Cuchilleros 17, 28005
+ 34 913 664 217
botin.es

Must-try
Goat stew at La Carmencita
One of the oldest *tabernas* in Madrid, La Carmencita opened in 1854 and became the haunt of some of Spain's literary greats. After falling into disrepair it was beautifully restored by food entrepreneur Carlos Zamora. Everything is made with organic ingredients sourced from small producers. Rafael de Bejes supplies the goat meat from the Cantabrian mountains for this traditional stew, a dish that perfectly embodies La Carmencita's no-nonsense approach.
*tabernalacarmencita.
wordpress.com*

Taste of tradition
—
Ancient cuisines thrive in Madrid's gastronomic melting pot. Look out for delicacies such as a crispy-squid sandwich, the beloved 'cocido madrileño' stew and 'criadillas' (testicles). For an informed food safari see María Arranz's essay on page 74.

Raw materials
—
Sala de Despiece does the basics well

Must-try

Tortilla with soft-shell crab at Juana La Loca

For the uninitiated, La Latina's endless selection of tapas bars and restaurants can be a little overwhelming. When in doubt, head to Juana La Loca, perched just across the road from Plaza Puerta de Moros. This lively spot is famous for its succulent, golden tortilla. For purists, the excess caramelised onion is sacrilege, but who says everyone has to follow the same recipe? Order it with the exquisite soft-shell crab – it's a match made in food heaven.

juanalalocamadrid.com

Tapas tour

As thousands flock to the El Rastro flea market on Sundays the surrounding 'tabernas' and 'tascas' fill up with hungry crowds. You can easily spend a day sampling tapas here as far as your stamina (and stomach) allows. If you want a quieter meal, visit mid-week.

(14) Sala de Despiece, Chamberí
Contemporary classic

Like nowhere else on the Spanish food scene, Sala de Despiece makes an impression as a brightly hued modern restaurant but then continues to seduce with its considered, playful exploration of the basic elements of Spanish food. Master chef Javier Bonet (*pictured, right*) and his team dissect the core ingredients of Spanish gastronomy – meat, seafood, vegetables – with an unembellished menu focusing on taste and technique that enthralls a loyal crowd.

This is exactly the type of eye-bulging experience that induces varying sounds of pleasure and usually leads to over-ordering. Meanwhile, next door, the Academia del Despiece delivers hi-tech nocturnal cooking courses, a combination of interactive projections and the chef's own unique insights.

Calle Ponzano 11, 28010
+ 34 917 526 106
academiadeldespiece.com

Chifa, Chamberí
Fantastic fusion

Be sure to book ahead for this popular hotspot, which owners Estanislao Carenzo and Pablo Giudice (the forces behind the nearby restaurant Sudestada, see page 39) have built into an innovative blend of Peruvian and Asian cooking. Located just north of the historic centre in a commercial district close to Nuevos Ministerios, its polished wooden interiors are a popular spot to explore the cuisine known as *chifa*, an exotic mix of Chinese and Peruvian.

Behind its corrugated aluminum exterior and elegant Helvetica signage, the small but invariably packed dining room is serviced by sharply attired waiters who buzz between kitchen and table. They deliver small tapas-style plates that pair fresh fish and delicate Asian flavours with Peruvian staples such as *choripán*, *tamales* and ceviche.
Calle Modesto Lafuente 64, 28003
+34 915 347 566

15

Ana La Santa, Las Letras
Taking care of business

Schedule a morning meeting at this newly created space inside Hotel ME. Restaurant group En Compañía de Lobos took over the vast ground floor in 2014, opting to divide the large space into several intimate settings.

The plant-filled library corner is the perfect spot for breakfast; the centuries-old *Teatro Español* (ideal for an open-air affair) and restaurant main floor provide a comfortable base for a relaxed working lunch. Do order some of the delectable side dishes – they'll be good for business.
Plaza Santa Ana 14, 28012
+34 917 016 013
restauranteanalasanta.com

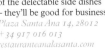

Ah, sweet churros – a dog's best friend

(19)
La Tasquita de Enfrente, Malasaña
Talking tripe

This slow-cooked classic has been serving a following of neighbours and clued-in visitors for more than half a century. Owner Juanjo López was an insurance executive before he tired of the number-crunching trade and took over his father's restaurant instead.

Generations of family recipes are cooked with the finest fresh produce, personally procured by López from a network of suppliers across the Iberian peninsula. If you truly want to eat like a local and try Madrid's beloved *callos* (tripe), this is the place to take the plunge.

The surrounding Malasaña neighbourhood is unrecognisable from when this restaurant opened five decades ago and López's team has contributed to the transformation, recently opening an old-fashioned Spanish *bocadillo* sandwich joint next door.
Calle de la Ballesta 6, 28004
+ 34 915 325 449
latasquitadeenfrente.com

(17)
La Mucca, Las Letras
Leisurely affair

This lively spot for a light bite is also a solid after-midnight dinner option. Located between the Prado Museum and Puerta del Sol, the kitchen is open all day (a luxury in Spain), ensuring a steady flow of diners to feast on *raciones* (try the *pimientos de padrón*). There is also an impressive cocktail list and Mexican beer-based drinks known as *micheladas*. Mismatched decor and a vibrant after-dark scene mean a trip to La Mucca, which has two other restaurants in the city, could see an early dinner stretch into the early hours.
Calle del Prado 16, 28014
+ 34 915 210 000
lamucca.es

(28)
Bosco de Lobos, Chueca
Immaculately Italian

Let's face it, you can't be feasting on *jamón ibérico* and Michelin-recommended molecular meals at every turn. This secluded Italian-flavoured restaurant is the best place to broaden your food horizons – if only as far as Italy.

Chef Max Colombo offers up a range of classics and the wooden deck is an ideal spot for an evening spritz. Hidden inside the restored College of Architects, the restaurant is surrounded by the manicured gardens of landscape architect Ana Esteve.
Colegio de Arquitectos, Calle Hortaleza 63, 28004
+ 34 915 249 464
encompaniadelobos.com

Spice of life
—
Muta Bar's menu changes on a regular basis

20
Diverxo, Chamartín
Michelin man

David Muñoz (*pictured*) is Spain's latest culinary *enfant terrible*, treating 40 diners a night to a sensory overload of Spanish-Asian cuisine that typically lasts four hours and includes rare ingredients sourced from around the globe. Madrid has a plethora of Michelin-starred restaurants and Diverxo can claim three stars all to itself, although this translates into a minimum six-week waiting period for a table.

Having achieved fortune and fame, Muñoz relocated his restaurant to the base of the NH Eurobuilding hotel. The eccentric space articulates his unique take on luxury dining but the food is where his personality really shines through: pioneering and rebellious, zealous yet methodical. Forgot to call ahead? Head to Muñoz's Asian street-food stall Streetxo at Calle Serrano's Gourmet Experience.
Calle Padre Damián 23, 28036
+34 915 700 766
diverxo.com

21
Muta Bar, Chamberí
Diverse palate

unable to find

Madrileños have something of a tendency to pounce on everything new for a few frenzied months before moving en masse to the next big opening. However, chef Javier Bonet has come up with a novel way to combat the transient trend, opening this transforming restaurant a short pace from his other popular venue Sala de Despiece.

Muta (which means "mutate" in Spanish) embraces change with a new regionally themed menu every few months, which has previously ranged from Brazilian street food to Balearic island delicacies. This laidback culinary laboratory embraces a sense of experimentation with a rotating roster of guest chefs. The furniture gets in on the act too, ready to be adapted to suit breakfast, lunch or dinner.
Calle Ponzano 10, 28010
+34 912 509 897
muta.bar

Latin fusion

Honouring tradition doesn't have to follow a rigid recipe. Navaja restaurant (Calle Valverde 42) specialises in Galician cuisine with a Peruvian punch, serving succulent octopus, fresh oysters and tangy ceviche to adoring diners each night.

② Celso y Manolo, Chueca
Tasca masters

Traditional *tascas* are resurgent in Madrid, tapping into a love for authentic food and informality. A *tasca* typically serves unfussy cuisine over a prominent bar and can be a loud, somewhat dated environment to eat in. Not so in this well-measured space, which is located in the vibrant Chueca district. Food entrepreneur Carlos Zamora offers a modern take on the concept yet ensures that a hearty helping of tradition makes it into every dish.

Tired legs should take note: this is not a case of standing room only. You will be pleased to hear that there are plenty of tables and chairs lining the walls. So sit back, relax and snack on all manner of tasty dishes, including *rabas* (small calamari) and a *cata de tomates* (tomato tasting plate), for as long as you please.

Calle Libertad 1, 28004
+34 915 318 079
tascacelsoymanolo.wordpress.com

㉓ Dstage, Las Salesas
Immersed in flavour

In 2014, the reborn Las Salesas district improved its culinary credentials when celebrated Basque chef Diego Guerrero (*pictured*) opened Dstage. A bespoke food experience allows diners to choose from a 10-course or 13-course degustation menu even before they have left home.

The chef, who left El Club Allard in 2013, wanted to step away from à la carte service, instead encouraging diners to roam around the space – including the kitchen – in an immersive experience of taste, sound and smell.

Calle Regueros 8, 28004
+34 917 021 586
dstageconcept.com

Must-try
Iberian pork ear salad
at Sudestada

Estanislao Carenzo has earned
a reputation as one of Madrid's
most scrupulous chefs, mixing
Spanish, Latin American and
Asian flavours at his restaurant
Sudestada. Some of the
Argentinian's creations require
so many ingredients and such
lengthy preparation that they
have redefined the term
"slow-cooked". The signature
salad of cured Iberian pork ear
with grapefruit, cauliflower,
shiso and kaffir lime leaf fuses
tradition with the avant garde
to create the perfect starter.
sudestada.eu

24
Casa Fidel, Malasaña
Tradition with a twist

Pairing traditional cooking with a
sharp eye for design has proved a
successful formula for Casa Fidel.
A backdrop of black-and-white
photography, fresh blooms and
industrial lighting sets a traditional
yet arty tone for this quiet spot, just
around the corner from the
commotion of Plaza San Ildefonso.

Popular with locals at breakfast,
the cooking comes into its own later
in the day with regional specialities
served with Spanish hospitality. The
zesty Andalusian *salmorejo* soup
and fresh flavours of the *txipirones
en su tinta* – stuffed baby squid in
ink – are highly recommended.
Calle del Escorial 6, 28004
+ 34 915 317 736

Pass the pig
———

In Spain 'jamón ibérico', from
pigs fed solely on acorns,
is a coveted comestible but
tough economic times mean
residents have tightened their
'jamón' budgets. In response
producers have turned into
retailers – their ventures
are well worth a visit for a
tasting session.

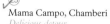

Mama Campo, Chamberí
Delicious detour

Part organic-food market, part restaurant, part Spanish designer showcase, Mama Campo brims with homegrown talent. Yes, it's off the beaten path but worth the trip as Madrid's tree-filled Plaza de Olavide is as authentic as the city gets. Chef Daniel Larios helps outsiders adapt to beloved local delicacies by reinterpreting traditional recipes such as *cocido Madrileño*: a traditional chickpea-based stew.

Proprietors Nacho Aparicio and David Yllera scoured the countryside for more than a year to source the best organic producers, and the same approach has been applied to the interior. About 50 designers have created a visceral feast with lampshades by Alvaro Catalán de Ocón, tables by Nikolas Piper and a plethora of other specially commissioned fittings.
Calle Trafalgar 22, 28010
+ 34 914 474 138
mamacampo.es

Use your loaf

One of the city's most coveted bakeries is Javier Marca's Panic in Conde Duque. Since it opened in 2014, fans have been lining up for loaves made by a talented team that revives classic techniques and tastes. High demand means getting in early for this crust is a must.

El Barril de Las Letras, Las Letras
Fresh off the boat

Despite being a landlocked city, Madrid takes its seafood seriously and the municipal fish market Mercamadrid is the biggest in Spain. El Barril de Las Letras casts its line far and wide, serving a boatload of regional recipes with the freshest ingredients.

El Barril's highlights include seared octopus with aioli and a modern take on paella served with seasonal vegetables and home-made breads. The split-level space has high ceilings as well as knowledgeable staff to help you select the pick of the catch.
Calle Cervantes 28, 28014
+ 34 911 863 632
barrildelasletras.com

Bakeries and sweet shops

01 **Mamá Framboise, Las Salesas:** This bakery-cum-café was created by talented pastry chef Alejandro Montes. The Asturian maestro has married natural ingredients with skilful glazing, which shines through in his cakes, pastries, macarons and chocolate bonbons.
mamaframboise.com

02 **Mistura Ice Cream, various locations:** Launched by a pair of entrepreneurs, Mistura scoops up ice cream with a sprinkle of swagger and plenty of fresh toppings. The duo were inspired by a "frozen stone" concept they saw in India; ice-cream lovers can mix fresh fruit and other treats into their favourite flavours.
misturaicecream.com

03 **Dray Martina, Las Salesas:** An altar-like cake stand sits at the rear laden with homemade creations such as a blueberry and gooseberry cheesecake. Be sure to try the apple and cherry crumble or the *helado Martina* – ice cream in a terracotta pot served with a surfeit of toppings and sprinkles.
draymartina.com

04 **Harina, Retiro:** Views of the iconic Puerta Alcalá gate are only one reason this high-end bakery has become such a popular spot. With its Provençal-style decor – think lavender pots and Tolix-style seating – and a breakfast of fresh breads and creative cakes (the chocolate and beetroot is a winner), this place will fuel you with energy at the start of a long day of urban exploration.
harinamadrid.com

Drinks
Perfect pours

La Bicicleta Café, Malasaña
Bespoke design

A cyclist pit-stop, co-working hotspot and reliable nightspot, La Bicicleta Café is not just a hub for the new generation of Malasaña's creatives: it's also a shining example of Madrid's social revival.

This prized location, on the edge of Plaza de San Ildefonso, lay empty for decades before young entrepreneurs Quique Arias and Tamara Marquése gave it a radical transformation. With good coffee on offer, this is a hive of activity at all hours – even Spain's fashionable young queen has dropped by to give it the royal seal of approval.
Plaza San Ildefonso 9, 28004
+34 915 329 742
labicicletacafe.com

Bodega La Ardosa, Malasaña
Drink in the history

A Madrid institution, the Bodega La Ardosa dates back to 1892. A miniature television stacked among the faded, dusty wall of bottles is perhaps the only clue to the fact that the world outside has changed in the century since.

Find yourself a perch among the ancient barrels and historic photos to enjoy the homemade vermouth or a heady red rioja. Sate your appetite with a serving of the *rabas de Cantabria* (crispy fried calamari), the sublime grilled artichokes and the legendary *tortilla de patatas*.
Calle Colón 13, 28004
+34 915 214 979
laardosa.es

① 1862 Dry Bar, Malasaña
Cocktail culture

Everything about this compact bar is intended as a mark of respect to the cocktail, from a name that symbolises the date that barman Jerry Thomas published the first book on how to mix drinks to the acumen on show as bar staff concoct up to 30 classic recipes.

Owner Alberto Martínez (*pictured*) hopes his customers leave appreciating the art of a well-poured cocktail as much as he does. If you're in the mood to debate the nuances of the ultimate Old Fashioned, 1862 opens early so there's plenty of time to pull up a stool and sermonise well into the evening.
Calle del Pez 27, 28004
+34 609 531 151

Don't look at me like that. This supply will last me at least a week

④
Kikekeller, Malasaña
Creative mix

As the sun goes down, pedestrians unfamiliar with this industrial façade often pass by with puzzled looks. If you didn't know any better, you might think Kikekeller was simply an extremely successful design shop that had forgotten to close for the night. Step inside and walk through the small door in the rear corner though and you will find an eccentrically furnished showroom turned bar.

Kike Keller once worked as a movie prop man but decided to turn his welding hand to crafting metallic furniture and designware. By night he and partner Celia transform the retail space into a vibrant nightspot playing subtle indie pop and serving well-made gin-tonics. If any of the fixtures catch your eye you're in luck: it's all available to buy.
Calle Corredera Baja de San Pablo 17, 28004
+34 915 228 767
kikekeller.com

⑤
El Amante, Sol
Secluded spot

This clandestine nightclub has a Stanley Kubrickian air of secret society about it. This is mainly due to its near-impenetrable door policy (which jars with Madrid's relaxed nightlife) but it's not impossible to get past the fortified mirrored entrance.

Once inside you will be rubbing one shoulder with an inebriated aristocrat as the other brushes

against a footloose Spanish actor. Weekends have a strict list-only door policy so make this a midweek visit or try to get on that sacred list by visiting ahead and underlining your *very* important credentials.
Calle Santiago 3, 28013

⑥
Bar Corazón, Malasaña
Clear the decks

Once a moribund Irish pub, this is now one of Malasaña's most eclectic haunts following a serious makeover by hospitality heavyweights Sergio Ochoa and Julián Lara. Ochoa redesigned the venue himself, opting for polished wood and a touch of taxidermy.

The drinks, and DJs spinning upbeat tunes, are the real draw though; don't be surprised if the lads and ladies on the decks step down to stir up the dancefloor themselves. Meanwhile, at the bar Ochoa's own beer label, Malasaña Pilsner, is thirstily embraced by proud *Malasañeros*.
Calle Valverde 44, 28004
+34 618 428 175

Top drinks

01 Vermouth: *Vermut*, as it's known locally, is currently experiencing a resurgence in the Spanish capital. Once the exclusive domain of the elderly, this classic concoction of wine, absinthe and distilled herbs is being lapped up by a younger generation as a more sophisticated aperitivo, in place of a simple *caña*. "Vermut de Grifo" signs are now brandished as a source of pride at the front of old watering holes such as Malasaña's rough-edged Casa Camacho.
+34 915 313 598

02 Tinto de Verano: That burgundy-coloured icy drink that you see every second person sipping isn't sangria: it's what Spaniards call "summer wine". This refreshing iced drink is a mix of red wine and lemon squash or *gaseosa* (sugared soda water) and is a staple of most drinks menus. We recommend pulling up a chair on the side terrace at Ana La Santa on Plaza de Santa Ana and ordering a cooling glass.
restauranteanalasanta.com

03 Maracuya Sour: While the gin-tonic is still the drink of choice for many *Madrileños*, some bars, such as La Pescaderia on Calle de la Ballesta, have been daring their customers with different, more exotic tipples. The Maracuya Sour is a passion fruit-flavoured pisco sour that has won legions of new followers. A strong, tangy kick makes it the perfect source of liquid courage before hitting a Madrid dancefloor.
lamucca.es

⑦
The Passenger, Malasaña
First-class cocktails

If you crave good music, a carefully mixed cocktail or just a creatively infused gin-tonic, hop aboard The Passenger bar. Stationed in the thriving Malasaña district, the long, narrow nightspot's interior has been modelled to look like a classic train carriage, complete with faux windows that are actually screens that project a neverending moving landscape.

Opened in 2012 by a group of innovative young entrepreneurs, the bar continues to pulsate with equal measures of energy and elegance; it's a winning formula that is also applied to the well-poured drinks.
Calle del Pez 16, 28004
+34 911 694 976

⑧
Martinez, Malasaña
Informal drinking den

Hidden behind Telefonica's vast Gran Via HQ, this laidback drinking parlour pours some of the city's best cocktails. Set inside a former tobacco seller, old wooden shop drawers that once housed cigars now hold botanicals used in the creation of experimental libations.

If you're feeling peckish, a selection of hams, cheeses and cakes provide accompaniment; friendly faces behind the bar will steer you in the right drinking direction. Amid an eclectic crowd and old-school atmosphere, slip onto a stool and enjoy one of the lemongrass-infused gin cocktails.
Calle del Barco 4, 28004
+34 910 802 683

Old-school bars

01 La Venencia, Las Letras: On a narrow street just a stone's throw from the Spanish parliament, this sherry bar has barely changed since its beginnings during the Spanish Civil War. The owners maintain a strong Republican spirit – not taking tips, for example (it's a socialist thing).
+34 914 297 313

02 Antigua Casa Ángel Sierra, Chueca: Chueca has gone from down-at-heel district to vibrant destination but the Antigua Casa Angel Sierra hasn't budged one bit since opening in 1917. It still serves natural ciders, vermouth on tap and an impeccable range of *banderillas*: tapas served on a small skewer.
+34 915 310 126

03 Bar Cock, Chueca: The panelled walls, art deco fixtures and fascinating history (it once served as an upmarket brothel) make this an atmospheric spot for an evening drink. The interior is augmented by a range of classic cocktails, while the back wall is adorned with portraits of the bar's namesake by prominent Spanish artists.
barcock.com

Steeped in history
Cocktails are relatively new to Madrid but the city has a long tradition of infusion. Narciso Bermejo's Macera Bar (Calle San Mateo 21) rekindles this ritual: gin, vodka and rum are infused in-house with fruit and botanicals. Turn your sip into a souvenir by buying a bottle to take home.

Late-night bars

01 Toni2, Chueca: One of the most endearing traits of the Spanish is their tendency to sing when under the influence. This ubiquitous propensity is on full display at the Toni2 piano bar, where the music keeps the endorphins and drinks flowing in equal measure. No, it's not karaoke; more a combo of a giant Spanish family Christmas celebration and a drunken *Kumbayah* campfire singalong.
toni2.es

02 Mauna Loa, Las Letras: Wet your beak with a cocktail at this subterranean *tiki* bar steeped in Hawaiian kitsch. Mauna Loa is brimming with so many quirks that you'll have plenty to talk about as you sip from metre-long straws out of a communal ceramic volcano (if you're into that sort of thing). Hold on to your hats: a flock of bold, free-flying budgerigars add a dose of avian anarchy.
+34 914 297 062

03 Laidy Pepa, Chueca: One of the few places in Madrid to hold the almost-extinct late-night licence, this family-run establishment attracts a motley crowd looking to *tomar el ultimo* (take the last drink). They also eat beloved delicacies – such as lentils, *callos* and *spaguetis* – and generally be merry: a piano and guitar are on hand to complement the gleefully embraced open-mic policy. It opens late (01.00) and closes early (08.00) – or vice versa, depending on your body clock.
Calle San Lorenzo 5, 28004

Cafés
Freshly brewed

Toma Café, Malasaña
Espresso delivery

The expansion of this espresso bar in Malasaña reflects Madrid's still nascent but growing coffee culture. The undeniable pioneers of this caffeine revolution are Patricia Alda Díaz and Santiago Rigoni, a Spanish-Argentinian couple whose upbeat attitude is suitably conducive to purveying caffeinated beverages.

They have transformed their welcoming café into a non-stop operation that now includes a select menu with Asian and Latin American undertones and an extremely talented Persian pastry chef. Avocado cake, anyone?
Calle de la Palma 49, 28004
+ 34 917 025 620
tomacafe.es

Two more coffee shops

01 Bianchi Kiosko Caffe, Malasaña: There's not much room to sit down in Sandro Bianchi's postage stamp-sized espresso bar but his coffee warrants a walk-by for a takeaway cup. Sip it in nearby Plaza San Ildefonso.
Calle San Joaquín 6, 28004

02 Coffee & Kicks, Sol: After finishing his studies and deciding he didn't want to return to his hometown of León, Guillermo Lasalle opened this coffee spot behind the Plaza Callao. It is influenced by his dual love of rare trainers and a strong *ristretto*.
Calle Navas de Tolosa 6, 28013

Rooftop bars
High society

① **Azotea del Círculo, Cortes**
All-round ability

Atop the historic Círculo de Bellas Artes, this rooftop terrace provides views of the city's terracotta-tiled buildings. Yet it took many years for someone to take the initiative and turn the space into a fully functioning bar and restaurant.

The new Tartán Roof restaurant serves a combination of traditional and modern Spanish food while a separate bar prepares a mean mojito. A token entry fee is required to get up top but on a warm evening, this elevated location includes plenty of spots to sprawl out and drink under the stars.
Calle Marqués de Casa Riera 2, 28014
azoteadelcirculo.com

② **La Cocina de San Antón, Chueca**
Market leader

Chueca's Antón Martín market is crowned with this smart rooftop terrace. The white marble bar serves up drinks to satisfy the mixed crowd's thirst, while the upbeat restaurant is divided into two spaces.

The interior is ideal for a more intimate dinner, while the exterior terrace sits under a canopy that includes sprinklers spraying a cool mist. If you're feeling adventurous, buy some fresh meat or fish from the market downstairs, bring it up to the kitchen and a talented chef will cook it for you.
Calle de Figueroa 24, 28004
+34 913 300 294
lacocinadesananton.com

Don't mind me, I'm just resting between cocktails

③ **La Terraza del Hotel Óscar, Chueca**
Moving on up

Anyone looking to climb up to this pristine white rooftop oasis needs a little insider knowledge first. The Hotel Óscar's rooftop is only available to paying customers before 18.00 (€20 will grant you use of the small pool and a sun lounger, with a towel and drink to boot). But as evening sets in you will need to turn on the charm before reaching for your wallet.

Flash a smile to the hotel receptionist, who should promptly facilitate your ascent in the lift. Once at the top, stake out the best spot to watch the sunset.
Plaza de Vázquez de Mella 12, 28004
+34 917 011 173
oscar.room-matehotels.com

Food markets
Fresh thinking

Trips to food markets are enshrined in the Spanish tradition but in Madrid these old-fashioned grocers have evolved into hubs of gastronomic excellence. The iron-hued ~~Mercado de San Miguel~~ is the most gleaming (and well known) example of this new model but following years of public investment – and a few bold private initiatives – there is now a thriving new network of compact inner-city food halls to bite into. Rookie cooks can be found alongside renowned chefs as longstanding greengrocers and delicatessens serve up fodder for residents' food baskets.

no longer at the address

El Huerto de Lucas, Las Salesas
Market garden

It is easy to lose a morning inside the dreamy walls of El Huerto de Lucas, tucked in a quiet central backstreet. The "Garden of Lucas" is the brainchild of chef Javier Muñoz Calero, who cultivates the harvest from his orchard to help supply the marketplace and canteen.

Feast on a quinoa *taboulé* or steak tartare at the café's wooden tables and chairs that sit beneath potted plants draped from the rafters. Before leaving, explore the sea of organic produce supplied by the other sellers that border the open-plan marketplace.
Calle San Lucas 13, 28004
+ 34 915 135 466
elhuertodelucas.com

Mercado de San Ildefonso, Malasaña
Street spirit

Set on the Fuencarral retail strip, this gastronomic experience mixes street-food atmosphere with a comfortable indoor infrastructure. The three-level space brims with noise as people tuck into delicious portions of mainly Spanish food, from the rich taste of *jamón ibérico* to fried sardines or succulent tortillas with prawns and spinach.

The small stalls lining the walls have been designed to rekindle a bygone era, modelled on the outdoor markets that occupied the neighbouring Plaza San Ildefonso. The colourful spread of classic cuisine, modern morsels and Spanish wine is best savoured on the hidden outdoor terrace.
Calle Fuencarral 57, 28004
mercadodesanildefonso.com

THREE STALLS
01 Gambas: Huelva prawns
02 Granja Malasaña: egg tortillas
03 Arturo Sanchez: Iberian ham

③
Platea, Salamanca
Theatre of food

Built inside the vast former Carlos
III cinema, this theatrical gourmet
leisure centre opened in 2014 after
an investment of €60m. The dining
hall is anchored by six restaurants
while smaller retailers deliver
lighter fare of seafood, stews and
burgers. At night the gastronomic
spectacle turns into a full sensory
experience of art, music and dance.
Calle Goya 5-7, 28001
+34 915 770 025
plateamadrid.com

THREE STALLS
01 As Bateas: oysters
02 Mama Framboise: desserts
03 Arriba: restaurant by Ramón
    Freixa

④
Mercado de Antón Martín,
Lavapiés
Food and flamenco

With the percussion from the
renowned Amor de Dios Flamenco
school providing an authentic
soundtrack from above, the
Antón Martín Market is a thriving
juxtaposition of the old and new.
  The market is shared by
traditional charcuterie merchants,
fishmongers and fruit sellers as
well as a growing population of
miniature market restaurants
that include one of Madrid's best
Japanese venues, Yokaloka, and the
zesty Mexican Cutzamala. Market
management also brightens up
the space by enlisting artists to
reinterpret some of the shopfronts.
Calle Santa Isabel 5, 28012
+34 913 690 620
mercadoantonmartin.com

THREE STALLS
01 Yokaloka: Japanese restaurant
02 Cutzamala: Mexican food
03 Establishments Romero:
    'jamón ibérico'

⑤
Mercado de San Antón, Chueca
Global gastronomy

This refurbished market has helped
reinvigorate the Chueca district.
The petite ground floor with 22
stalls offers a gourmet excursion
through the finest grocers from
Spain and abroad. On offer are
exotic meats and poultry, fish,
baguettes, regional mushrooms
and quality olive oils.
  One floor above, a mezzanine
level provides a degustation of
small tapas with both Iberian and
international flavours. There is
usually standing room only so if it's
too busy, head upstairs to restaurant
La Cocina de San Antón. The
rooftop bar is an ideal spot for an
afternoon aperitif.
Calle Augusto Figuero 24, 28004
+34 913 300 730
mercadosananton.com

THREE STALLS
01 Octavio Delicatessen: cheese
02 Murua Oleoteca: olive oil
03 La Cocina de San Antón:
    sit-down Spanish restaurant

Retail
—— Flash the cash

Menswear
Modern couture

From Andrés Gallardo and Helena Rohner to Masscob and Loewe, we've visited our favourite Spanish designers and shops. The capital's retail scene is marked by polar opposites that stretch from fast-fashion giants (Zara, anyone?) to small wonders such as bespoke shoemaker Glent in Salamanca.

We've avoided the big chains – you most probably know them already anyway – and concentrated solely on smaller retailers. That might be a multibrand menswear shop selling predominantly Scandinavian and Brit offerings (Goyo Otero's Sportivo) or a tiny family-owned glove shop and manufacturer that has been in business since 1896 (Guantes Luque). And in case you need to order thank-you flowers, we've got that covered too.

①
Mini, Conde Duque
Seriously playful

Oscar Gala's small and aptly named shop fits perfectly into Madrid's artsy Conde Duque neighbourhood. Gala has styled loyal customers since the early 2000s and says he has developed a "refined focus on smaller independent brands with proven quality such as Barena, Oliver Spencer and Steve Mono".

An eccentric collection of taxidermy along with Persian rugs and cowboy-themed wallpaper accentuates Mini's playful yet elegant approach to fashion. Barena chinos and Engineered Garments blazers are punctuated by more casual touches such as trainers and baseball caps, a functional marriage of formal with casual that typifies the owner's relaxed attitude to bringing together this smart collection.
Calle Limón 24, 28015
+ 34 915 480 835
minishopmadrid.com

TOP PICKS
01 Shoes by Oliver Spencer
02 'Rampin' chinos by Barena
03 Floral-pattern shirt by Gitman Brothers Vintage
04 Blazer by Engineered Garments
05 Sweater by Our Legacy

④

Sportivo 2, Las Salesas
Northern exposure

The second outpost of Goyo Otero's Sportivo opened in early 2015 as a much-anticipated addition to the original shop on Calle Conde Duque. This larger space on Calle Justiniano leans heavily towards UK and Scandinavian brands such as Han Kjøbenhavn, Andersen-Andersen, Norse Projects, Hentsch Man, Margaret Howell, Oliver Spencer and Sunspel.

"I go on buying trips regularly to keep our selection up to date," says Otero, who has been in the business for more than 20 years.
Calle Justiniano 14, 28004
+ 34 913 082 135
gruposportivo.com

③

Bunkha, Malasaña
Taking centre stage

"The shop is a refuge of beauty and comfort," says Bunkha's Brazilian founder Luiz Lobao, who has lived in Madrid for more than 15 years and opened his shop in 2008. Evoking the mystique of the theatre in its interior, the set designer and costumier's boutique thrives on difference. "The idea is to offer wearable contemporary brands that are less known in Spain," he says.

Bunkha's racks are filled with international womenswear but the shop is also a must for its menswear selection, from Uniforms for the Dedicated to Commune de Paris.
Calle Santa Bárbara 6, 28004
+ 34 915 220 950
bunkha.com

②

Eduardo Rivera, Chueca
Layered approach

When Eduardo Rivera (*pictured*) began searching for knitwear and stretchy cottons to tailor men's jackets, fabric suppliers were bewildered. Now his eponymous brand adorns four shopfronts across the city and his Spanish-made collection of jackets is adored for both style and comfort.

"Before I sell a new item I wear it to check the fit and the feel," says Rivera, who still lives within walking distance of his main shop on Calle Clavel. The store also stocks a full complement of his shoes and knitwear.
Calle Clavel 4, 28004
+ 34 915 229 350
eduardorivera.es

Yes, my fashion needs extend beyond a neckerchief

⑤
Glent, Salamanca
Personal footwear design

Time-honoured craftsmanship
goes into the making of Glent's
bespoke footwear but it is the
specially designed 3D-measuring
system that makes sure every shoe
fits perfectly. Step into the shop
on Calle de Jorge Juan to see how
the brand's 16 elegant models can
be personalised for each customer,
choosing from 15 types of leather
in 30 tones.

"The final design is in the hands
of the clients," says founder and
head designer Carlos Baranda.
"They can choose the colour and
the type of leather, the material for
the sole, the stitching – even the
colour of the laces."

Featuring an additional cork
layer for insulation and comfort, all
shoes are made in the north of the
country using leather sourced from
the best tanneries in Spain, France
and Italy.
Calle de Jorge Juan 14, 28001
+34 914 315 581
glentshoes.com

Noble tradition
Update your
look with a
clean-cut
classic

Garcia Madrid, Malasaña
Head-to-toe wardrobe

Clean and contemporary was how
founding partner and creative
director Manuel Garcia envisioned
his menswear brand's shop, which
was established in 2006.

From merino wool suits to
chunky knitwear and Italian
leather shoes, Garcia's space on
Corredera Baja de San Pablo
offers head-to-toe gents' clothing
with an emphasis on modern
tailoring firmly rooted in traditional
techniques. Pop in when you feel
the need to update any part of
your wardrobe.
Corredera Baja de San Pablo 26,
28004
+34 915 220 521
garciamadrid.com

An owl
can never
have
enough
bow ties

Womenswear
Bijou treasure troves

①
Sin Clon Ni Son, Malasaña
Old-style hideaway

Small boutiques have prospered in the alleys and quaint squares beyond the clamour of Fuencarral, Malasaña's big-brand high street; Sin Clon Ni Son is one that's certainly worth a visit.

Opened in 2010 by Carlos Pérez and his husband Gerardo Olaverry, the two floors of this former haberdashery act as a one-stop shop for womenswear and accessories. Treasures from Nordic heavyweights Swedish Hasbeens and Sandqvist sit alongside Spanish heroes such as Maians and Lucuix.
Plaza 2 de Mayo 10, 28004
+34 915 227 815
sinclonnison.com

TOP PICKS
01 Jewellery by Lucuix
02 Gloves by Santacana
03 Bags by Beatriz Furest
04 Shoes by Maians
05 Sunglasses by Waiting
     For The Sun

②
Masscob, Salamanca
Mid-price womenswear

Launched in 2003 by couple Marga Massanet and Jacobo Cobián, Masscob offers relaxed, beautifully designed women's pieces that are fairly priced. It's a rare find on the Spanish high street, which mostly offers either fast fashion or exclusive high-end brands with little in between.

Masscob actually has two shops: the original space in its native La Coruña and a roomy space on Madrid's cul-de-sac Puigcerdà, selling its entire collection of printed tops, lace-detailed shirts, slick dresses and tailored suits.
Calle Puigcerdà 2, 28001
+34 914 358 596
masscob.com

③
Malababa, Las Salesas
Dispensing accessories

Pharmacist-turned-designer Ana Carrasco opened Malababa's first shop on Calle Lagasca in 2010 after turning her hobby into an internationally renowned accessories brand. Today her leather bags, shoes and jewellery are sold in two Madrid stores.

You can witness the work in progress at the workshop close to the Calle Santa Teresa outpost, where craftsmen carefully dye leather for Malababa's bags and cut the architecturally inspired patterns for an accessories range that includes wallets, belts and jewellery.
Calle Santa Teresa 5, 28004
+34 912 035 990
malababa.com

④
Loewe, Gran Vía-Chueca
In the bag

When it comes to luxury, craftsmanship and unrivalled expertise with leather, high-end brand Loewe has been Spain's pride and glory for nearly two centuries. The historic shop on Gran Vía, designed by architect Francisco Ferrer Bartolomé, opened in 1939. Today it sells collections that include opulent silks and a full range of ready-to-wear men's and women's clothing alongside bags and wallets.

On the underground level is Galería Loewe, a space that is dedicated to the history of the brand. It showcases some signature pieces and leather-working tools used to construct the sought-after bags through the years. With a respect for its legacy, Loewe continues to manufacture its precious leather goods in the Spanish capital.
Gran Vía 8, 28013
+ 34 912 004 490
loewe.com

The down Loewe

The reputation of this well-established brand is growing apace with nine shops across Madrid and boutiques in 16 other Spanish cities. Loewe's ever-impressive range of clothing and accessories can also be found in 32 countries such as the UK, Japan and Mexico.

⑤
Helena Rohner, La Latina
Sparkling selection

Helena Rohner (*pictured*) sells her unique tableware and porcelain jewellery out of a snug showroom on the cobbled Calle Almendro. Pure lines and simple shapes come out of the hands of the Canary Islands-born designer, whose signature pieces combine traditional materials such as gold and silver with surprising details made from porcelain or wood. Rohner has also joined forces with creative minds such as Andrés Gallardo and David Delfín in order to put together more eclectic jewellery lines.

In recent years Rohner has gone beyond jewellery and has collaborated with established names such as Georg Jensen, Kahler and Bodum y Munio to produce intricate tableware, lamps and candle holders in stoneware, wood and porcelain.
Calle del Almendro 4, 28005
+ 34 913 657 906
helenarohner.com.es

⑥
Pez, Las Salesas
Feminine wiles

Patricia de Salas and Beatriz
Mezquíriz (*pictured, De Salas on
left*) opened their womenswear
shop Pez in 2004. "We wanted to
combine a more elegant European
style with New York-inspired
bohemian touches," says Mezquíriz.
   The boutique sells bags by the
in-house Pez label as well as shirts
by Equipment, dresses by Masscob
(*see page 51*) and flats by Ball Pagès.
Since 2010 the duo have run nearby
men's outlet Pez Chico, home to
clothes and accessories by Golden
Goose, Homecore, Melinda Gloss
and Hence.
*Calle de Regueros 15, 28004
+ 34 913 106 677
pez-pez.es*

When it comes to
shopping there's
no such thing as
a flying visit

Mixed retail
Concept stores

① Rughara and Casa Quiroga,
Malasaña
Double whammy

Vanesa Serrano (*pictured*) founded
Rughara in 2012, followed in 2014
by neighbouring Casa Quiroga.
The shops showcase Spanish decor,
accessories and clothing, with a few
Danish designs and some Latin
American artwork added.

Rughara features textiles by
Maria Roch from Denmark and
Spanish brand Batabasta, while
Casa Quiroga has everything
from vintage furniture to shoes by
Spanish brand Magro Cardona.
*Calle Corredera Alta de San Pablo
1 and 2, 28004
Casa Quiroga: + 34 910 703 797;
Rughara: + 34 910 116 565
rughara.com*

② La Fábrica, Las Letras
Looking literate

La Fábrica had already been running as a publishing house and art gallery for 18 years when, in 2013, a café and concept store got some room in the expanded two-floor space. Spot the shop's bright red awning in a quiet alley just behind the busy Paseo del Prado.

Gargantuan photo books and art titles fill the shelves, while the rest of the space is taken up by china, arty T-shirts, Spanish wine and flowers. "We like the good life and we think culture and food are part of that," says La Fábrica's María Peláez. Despite the shop's Nordic-looking interior, Spanish artists produce most of the homeware, stationery and accessories on display. "We try to promote people who are well known abroad but don't have as much space here," adds Peláez.
Calle Alameda 9, 28014
+ 34 912 985 546
lafabrica.com

TOP PICKS
01 Jewellery by Helena Rohner
02 Porcelain animals by Sargadelos
03 Bags by Steve Mono
04 Photo prints by La Fábrica
05 Olive oil by Tot Oli

③ El Imparcial, La Latina
Hungry for culture

Ascend the palatial marble staircase and you'll find yourself amid the clang of crockery and rustle of magazines. The site, once home of newspaper *El Imparcial*, was chosen by co-founder Ignacio Rodriguez to open a Madrid-inspired restaurant, shop and gallery.

You'll find everything from *patatas bravas* to art books about Spanish designers and painters. "Our philosophy is to create the things that we'd like to see, eat, watch or read," says Rodriguez.
Calle Duque de Alba 4, 28012
Restaurant reservations:
+ 34 917 958 986;
Shop: + 34 914 293 511
elimparcialmadrid.com

④ Isolée, Salamanca
Ever-changing edit

Inspired by the likes of Liberty, Bergdorf Goodman and Le Bon Marché, Jose L Robles and Rodrigo Menendez launched their first Isolée concept store in 2005. Beginning with a restaurant, a small selection of designer clothing and a cosmetics range, Isolée has since become a favourite fixture on Madrid's luxury-retail scene. A second, smaller space opened in Chueca in 2007.

"Our success is down to the fact that our shops and collections are always changing," says Robles who, along with Menendez, travels the globe on a regular basis in order to bring in the latest trends for customers to choose from. The owners also make a point of supporting home-grown talent such as Dear Tee and Guille García-Hoz.
Calle de Claudio Coello 55, 28001
+ 34 902 876 136

TOP PICKS
01 Vintage pieces from Le Coq Sportif
02 Clothing from Dear Tee
03 Chocolates from Pancracio
04 Ceramics from Guille García-Hoz
05 Fragrances from Ramón Monegal

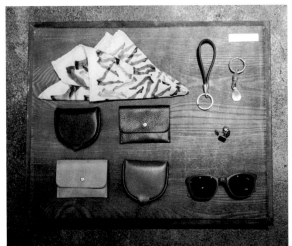

Homeware
Inspirational design

①
Modernario, Las Letras
One of a kind

Owner Julio Montero Melchor
(*pictured*) has been filling his
beautifully stocked shop for a
decade, amassing an impressive
collection of the great names in
20th-century European furniture
design. Gio Ponti, Angelo Lelli,
Hans Wegner, Charles and Ray
Eames and Niels Moller are all
represented here and Melchor
is always on hand to explain the
virtues of quality furniture from
Scandinavia and western Europe.
  "Modernario captures a great
moment in European creativity,
when building furniture was a team
effort between engineers, scientists
and cabinet makers," says Melchor.
Here you will find unique coffee
and cocktail tables, chairs and
sideboards, while a selection of
lamps illuminate the space and a
second showroom is located a few
steps away on Calle Moratin.
Calle de Santa María 20, 28014
+34 913 697 678
modernario.es

② Batavia, Las Salesas
Worldly goods

Carlos Alonso fell in love with furniture design while working in Indonesia as an engineer. He set up his business in 1996 to introduce Madrid to his favourite pieces from around the world.

While Alonso's penchant for rattan and teak is evident in the dressers, dining tables and lounge chairs on show, this shop in the city centre is also replete with well-known brands such as Eames, Artek and Hay. "We mix pieces from different aesthetics, materials, origins and ages," says branch manager David Pastor.
Calle Serrano Arguita 4, 28004
+ 34 915 942 233
batavia.es

③ Espacio Brut, Las Salesas
Form and function

Design shops have been springing up in Las Salesas and a stand-out is Espacio Brut, a studio, shop and gallery run by furniture designers Braulio Rodríguez and José Cámara (*pictured, Cámara on left*). The couple's pieces are inspired by Danish functionalism with hints of Bauhaus and De Stijl.

"Our designs are hand-crafted to last a lifetime," says Rodríguez. The duo are also interior designers and sell brands such as Finnish glassware by Iittala, shelves by String and design and fashion publications such as *Apartamento* and *032c*.
Calle Pelayo 68, 28004.
+ 34 910 258 963
espaciobrut.com

I recommend refuelling every half an hour

④
Woody Metal, La Latina
New lease of life

Home to some of the oldest
purveyors of even older furniture
and bric-a-brac, Madrid's
traditional Rastro district is in
the grip of generational change.
Among the new wave of young
Spaniards adding fresh colour
to the neighbourhood are Alicia
Sonlleva, Fichi Lazareno (*both
pictured, right*) and Julian Prieto,
whose shop on the iconic main
strip bills itself as a *sastrería de
muebles* ("tailor of furniture").

The trio scour Europe for the
best vintage pieces and skilfully
restore them to their former glory.
The shop often comes to life with
a DJ or live music. "Everyone
talks about the crisis but our main
challenge is to make sure we're
having fun," says Sonlleva. "It's the
reason we started the business and
we don't want to lose sight of this."
*Calle de la Ribera de Curtidores
19, 28005
+ 34 912 594 254
woodymetal.com*

(5)
Do Design, Las Salesas
Home is where the heart is

After studying in Finland, Lucía Ruiz-Rivas (*pictured*) returned to Madrid in 2011 to set up home accessories and design shop Do Design in the well-heeled Las Salesas neighbourhood. Tucked away between the Alonso Martínez and Chueca Metro stations, the shop's serene atmosphere allows for a relaxed shopping experience.

"I search for modern things with a traditional feel; things made from wood, porcelain, ceramics and natural fibres," says Ruiz-Rivas. Among her selection are notebooks by Japanese stationery company Midori, hand-woven baskets made by an artisan in southern Spain and brushes from Sweden's Iris Hantverk. Besides stocking up on her favourite global brands, Ruiz-Rivas has started collaborating with Spanish artists and her shop holds bimonthly art exhibitions. "I want this to be a place that inspires people and that is open to collaboration between disciplines."
Calle de Fernando VI 13, 28004
+ 34 913 106 217
dodesign.es

TOP PICKS
01 Traveler's Notebooks by Midori
02 Cotton pieces by Khadi and Co
03 Homeware by Linge Particulier
04 Sweaters by La Paz
05 Stationery by Gonjang

Lucía Ruiz-Rivas's favourite shops

01 Panta Rhei, Malasaña
An exceptional book collection.
panta-rhei.es
02 Masscob, Salamanca
Home-grown clothing brand.
masscob.com
03 Pez, Las Salesas
His and hers fashion.
pez-pez.es

(6)
Nikolas Piper, Las Salesas
Metallic taste

"I only work under commission and craftsmanship is key to my work," says German-born Nikolas Piper in his furniture studio, set in a row of discreet shops on Calle Justiniano. He established his business in 2005 after learning metallurgy from renowned blacksmith Antonio Bonet. It's a skill Piper continues to employ, evidenced by the coffee tables, chaises and shelves throughout the showroom.

Piper enjoys juxtaposing bronze, aluminium and steel against organic materials such as salvaged wood. As many of the pieces are too bulky for Madrid's visitors to fit into their suitcases, Piper handily provides international shipping. Otherwise, there are more manageable items such as table lamps, woven baskets and card-holders that would make a striking addition to any home.
Calle de Justiniano 7, 28004
+ 34 913 199 549
nikolaspiper.com

(7)
Tiempos Modernos, Ópera
European union

This was one of the first shops in Madrid to focus on contemporary design. It was opened by Carmen Palacios in 1988, who later teamed up with Portuguese antiquarian Bento Figueira. Specialising in the period from 1930 to 1980, the space is stacked with lampshades, ornaments and furniture sourced during scouting trips across Europe.

"We strive to bring refined objects to Spain made from the highest-quality woods," Figueira says. "Each piece is painstakingly restored before taking its place in the showroom."
Calle Arrieta 17, 28013
+ 34 915 428 594
tiempos-modernos.com

⑧
Concha Ortega, Las Letras
Restoring faith

Skilled furniture restorer Conchega
Ortega (*pictured*) oversees two
furniture and designware spaces
on Calle Moratin in Las Letras,
Madrid's renowned design district.
It's not unusual to see her dashing
between shops as she moves pieces
from one space to the other.

Ortega's furniture restoration
workshop and showroom, with its
beautiful turquoise-tiled façade, was
once home to a publishing house.
Expect a range of 18th-century
antiques, colourful 20th-century
furniture and an extensive collection
of vintage graphic-design pieces.
Calle Moratin 14A, 28014
+ 34 914 292 305
conchaortega.es

Specialist retail
Treasures and extras

①

Ecoalf, Las Salesas
Salvage squad

Founded by Javier Goyeneche,
Ecoalf makes products that look
and feel just as good as non-
recycled items. In a minimalist
space (even the interior is made
from recycled materials) you'll
find multicoloured flip-flops made
from tyres alongside swimming
trunks, trench coats and backpacks
that were once abandoned fishing
nets and plastic bottles.

"We believe in sustainable
fashion that makes a difference,"
says Goyeneche. Meanwhile,
new technology allows the
brand to create yarn from used
coffee grounds.
Calle Hortaleza 116, 28004
+ 34 917 374 108
ecoalf.com

③

Guantes Luque, Sol
Hands on

Small family-owned businesses are
slowly becoming the ruling retailers
of post-crisis Madrid and among
them is Guantes Luque, a glove
shop and manufacturer that has
been in business since 1886. Álvaro
Ruiz keeps the tiny atelier afloat
by producing small batches of his
designs to ensure steady sales.

Today customers can take their
pick from leather, cotton or lace
gloves in a variety of colours. Ruiz
also takes special orders for film and
TV productions and has even been
known to produce his wares for
European royals.
Calle de Espoz y Mina 3, 28012
+ 34 915 223 287

①
Antigua Casa Crespo, Malasaña
Best foot forward

Entering Antigua Casa Crespo,
Madrid's most famous espadrille
shop, is like walking into the past.
The shop fittings date back to
1836 when the business, now run
by fourth-generation owner Maxi
Garbayo (*pictured, on left*), was
founded. Initially Casa Crespo
specialised in selling straw, ropes
and simple sandals. Today its
craftsmen make and sell espadrilles
of various styles and colours.

"It is the only espadrille store
in Madrid with its own factory,"
says Garbayo, whose shoes
continue to be made in the village
of Cervera del Río Alhama. "The
greatest happiness is to see pleased
clients who come back every year
because they love and appreciate
our shoes." With hundreds
of models on display, regular
customers aren't about to get
bored any time soon.
Calle Divino Pastor 29, 28004
+ 34 915 215 654
antiguacasacrespo.com

④
Margarita Se Llama Mi Amor, Las Salesas
Flower power

These two Margarita Se Llama Mi Amor flower shops are perched next to each other in Las Salesas. The seasonal blooms from Spanish and international growers contrast beautifully with the shops' clean white interiors.

Founders Tina Rubio (*pictured*) and Juan Arena Rico named the venture after Ramon Fernandez's 1961 film *Daisy is Called my Love*. Ask one of five florists to wrap their pick for you; tulips and peonies are a couple of favourites.

Calle de Fernando VI 9, 28004
+34 910 259 809
margaritasellamamiamor.
wordpress.com

⑤
Farmacia Deleuze Isasi, Conde Duque
Treat yourself

With its wood-panelled entrance, sparkling chandeliers and ornate interiors, the Farmacia Deleuze Isasi is one of the oldest shops in the city. Resembling a royal drawing room rather than a chemist, the elaborate gilded rococo decor has been lovingly looked after and the interiors restored since the shop opened in 1780 under the name "Botica de San Bernardo".

Its back office has played host to meetings of intellectuals and artists throughout the centuries, as well as welcoming men of science, who, in the days of King Carlos III, concocted herbal remedies and elaborate ointments. Porcelain jars from the Buen Retiro factory still adorn its niches and there is a wide variety of drugs and tinctures on offer. There is also an array of beauty and care products for skin and hair.

Calle de San Bernardo 39, 28015
+34 915 420 913

Roaring trade
———
Another pharmacy worth a visit is Farmacia León on Calle León in Las Letras, which dates back to the end of the 17th century. Marvel at its façade, covered in traditional white-and-blue tiles depicting medicinal icons and a rather stern-looking lion.

Cane curios
—
Animal heads range from rhino to buffalo

⑥
Javier S Medina Artesano, Malasaña
Cane and able

"When I was little I used to see my father playing with all these worthless objects and make something beautiful and original out of them, so I guess I have it in my veins," says Javier Sánchez Medina (*pictured*), who hails from Extremadura in southern Spain.

Medina adopted the region's tradition of cane workmanship (the plant stem as opposed to the walking aid) and transformed an old garage in Malasaña into a studio-cum-shop. From here he makes and sells his beautiful creations, from quirky decorative animal heads to intricately woven mirror frames. He also makes the rounds to deliver his creatures to shops and bars that hang his handiwork on their walls. Stop by to watch him work and snap up the perfect souvenir.
Calle el Escorial 28, 28004
+ 34 666 009 240
javiersmedina.com

⑦

Radio City, Conde Duque
Get into the groove

This small but perfectly formed
record shop is well worth a visit.
With an emphasis on vinyl, this
space in the southwest corner of
Conde Duque showcases a strong
collection of records loosely grouped
by genre.

Rock, jazz and soul are
particularly well represented – with
records by artists ranging from
Bob Dylan and Sam Cooke to
Miles Davis – and there is a strong
collection of breakthrough acts.
There is also a fine choice of books
and magazines, plus artwork by
Spanish illustrator Sonia M Paredero.
Calle Conde Duque 14, 28015
+34 915 477 767
radiocitydiscos.com

⑧

Andrés Gallardo, Sol
Absolute gem

The new wave of Spanish
craftsmanship is epitomised
by Andrés Gallardo's intricate
jewellery. Made from porcelain
and 18-carat gold-plated brass, his
pieces are inspired by flora and
fauna and have already gained a
following in Japan, Hong Kong
and Russia, while in the UK they
sell at Paul Smith.

The designer has a shop near the
Tirso de Molina Metro station. In
2013 he added a handbag line to the
collection; made from organically
dyed leather, they are adorned with
whimsical porcelain inlays.
Calle Conde de Romanones 5, 28012
+34 911 569 110
andresgallardo.es

⑨

Óptica Toscana, Chueca
Eye on the prize

Founded back in 1992, Óptica
Toscana quickly established
itself as one of Madrid's most
fashionable eyewear emporiums.
More than two decades later and
the shop, now with additional
locations in Salamanca and
Barcelona, continues to stock a
roll call of sought-after spectacles
by new and veteran designers,
including the likes of Barton
Perreira and Mykita.

Glasses are filed in apothecary
drawers that line the walls in a nod
to the shop's storied past: seeds
and spices were sold here in the
19th century.
Calle Hortaleza 70, 28004
+34 913 605 007
opticatoscana.com

TOP PICKS
01   Lemtosh by Moscot
02   Norton by Barton Perreira
03   Scarlet by Anne et Valentin
04   Bocca range by Face à Face
05   Mylon range by Mykita

Clear vision
—
Óptica Caribou is a
five-minute walk from
Óptica Toscana and houses
an equally impressive range
of specs. In addition to its
in-house designs, the shop
sells Paulino Spectacles
from Portugal and Persol
from Italy.

Bookshops
Page turners

① La Central, Sol
Bookseller with a twist

It's easy to lose track of time amid the myriad shelves at La Central: the downtown bookshop that opened in 2012 is housed within a 19th-century palace.

While bibliophiles are burying their noses in the pages of more than 80,000 titles in multiple languages, don't forget to take in the beautiful frescoes on the ceiling. Meanwhile, the central stairway features the names of 100 notable authors hidden within the seemingly random letters engraved on it. Once you've stocked up on reading matter, head to the attached restaurant and cocktail bar for refreshments.
Calle del Postigo de San Martín 8, 28013
+34 917 909 930
lacentral.com

As you can see, it's a matter of time before I'll be a 'tablao' terrier

Three more

01 Tipos Infames, Malasaña: This dynamic space was founded by three friends in 2010 to challenge the traditional concept of a bookshop. In addition to selling novels by independent publishers, Tipos Infames also offers wine-tasting sessions.
tiposinfames.com

02 La Fiambrera, Malasaña: Maite Valderrama and Ruth López-Diéguez channelled their passion for design and founded La Fiambrera ("Lunch Box") in 2015 on Calle del Pez. It's part design bookshop, part gallery and part café; customers can also peruse an array of homeware and knick-knacks while sipping a craft beer.
lafiambrera.net

03 Panta Rhei, Chueca: Specialising in art and design books, Panta Rhei on Hernán Cortés is the place to go to admire some beautiful titles. The shop has been in its current location since 2010 and the friendly owners, sisters Ingrid and Lilo Acebal Neu, make sure that customers are well looked after.
panta-rhei.es

Things we'd buy
—— Spanish mainstays

Intricate fans, porcelain tea sets, wooden animals and zingy chorizo: they all make it onto our Madrid shopping list. And as you can't leave Spain without a good *vermut* or a sample of the finest rioja, we sourced our bottles from the capital, where you can find some of the best wines and spirits the country has to offer.

There are also high-quality bags and coin purses by one of our favourite leather brands and, of course, a pair of hand-stitched espadrilles, without which no *Madrileño* wardrobe can be considered complete.

01 Sunglasses by Óptica Caribou
opticacaribou.com
02 Extra-virgin olive oil and Himalayan salt crisps by San Nicasio
sannicasio.es
03 Sherry from Petra Mora
petramora.com
04 Craft pilsner by Cerveza Malasaña from Palma Brew
palmabrew.com
05 Handmade braided hat by Alegría Industries
alegriaindustries.com
06 Hand-stitched silk scarf by Suturno
suturno.net
07 Extra-virgin olive oil by Núñez de Prado
deprado.eu
08 *Medalla de Plata* by Wild Honey from Radio City
radiocitydiscos.com
09 Preserves from Petra Mora
petramora.com
10 Tinned fish by Conservas Ortiz
conservasortiz.com
11 Rioja Bordón by Bodegas Franco-Españolas
francoespanolas.com
12 Vermut Negre by Casa Mariol
casamariol.com
13 Spanish rice by Fallera from Supercor
supercor.es
14 Turrón by 1880
turron1880.com
15 Canvas tote with leather handles by Steve Mono
stevemono.com
16 Womenswear by Masscob
masscob.com
17 Fragrance by Alvarez Gómez
alvarezgomez.com
18 Chorizo by Alejandro Miguel
grupoalejandromiguel.es
19 Chato wine glasses from Hostelvia
vicrila.com
20 *Chema Madoz: Masterpieces* photography book by La Fábrica
lafabrica.com
21 Porcelain tea set by Sargadelos
sargadelos.com
22 Wooden toy by Wodibow
wodibow.com

01 Chocolates from Pancracio
pancracio.com
02 Cosmetics by Natura Bissé
naturabisse.com
03 Fans from Casa de Diego
casadediego.info
04 Wooden candleholders
by Helena Rohner
helenarohner.com.es
05 Leather purses by Steve Mono
stevemono.com
06 Merino wool-and-silk blanket
by Teixidors *teixidors.com*

07 Films by Pedro Almodóvar
from Cine Doré
+34 913 691 125
08 "Madrid" lamp by Alvaro
Catalán de Ocón
catalandeocon.com
09 *Spain for the Foreigners*
from La Central
lacentral.com
10 Espadrilles
by Antigua Casa Crespo
antiguacasacrespo.com

12 essays
—— Texts and
the city

My essay is about
'carajillo' (hic)

Talking shop
Boutique boom

Spain's retail scene is blossoming again after the financial crisis. Madrid, home to both fresh independent brands and long-established names doing the right things well, is particularly fertile ground.

by Nelly Gocheva, Monocle

While scouting the cobbled streets of Madrid and hunting for hidden gems for this guide, one thing hit me bright and clear: retail – from the biggest players to independent small-scale ventures – is alive and kicking in this city. Whether it's the well-off Salamanca neighbourhood or the characterful backstreets of Las Letras, the capital is a labyrinth of shops with more and more smaller retailers supporting a new wave of Spanish craftsmanship and a focus on local design.

In its abundancy, Zara is to Spain what Starbucks is to the US. This is nowhere more evident than in the nation's capital: outlets by the Galicia-based retailer and its sister companies Massimo Dutti and Bershka are generously sprinkled across the Madrid *centro*. At the other end of the spectrum is Spanish luxury brand Loewe (*see page 52*) with its flagship shop in the heart of Madrid on Gran Vía, which includes an opulent fashion-meets-art Galería exhibition space. However, global fast-fashion chains and high-end brands aside, what surprises a returning visitor such as myself is the deepening diversification of local retail, much of which proudly waves the "Made in Spain" flag: evidence of the welcome return of entrepreneurial spirit to post-crisis Madrid.

Independent brands such as Masscob and Steve Mono have been impressing loyal customers with their much-treasured lines of women's clothing and leather bags respectively for successive seasons. But an increasing clutch of younger designers are making a name for themselves in the capital and beyond. Among them is Andrés Gallardo with an atelier-cum-shop (*see page 64*) in multicultural Tirso de Molina, a short walk from the city's epicentre: Puerta del Sol. Gallardo, whose handcrafted porcelain pendants are now sold at Paul Smith in London, joins a stable of designers who have been regenerating Spain's porcelain industry, adding a contemporary twist to a centuries-old tradition.

The figurines from cherished Spanish ceramics brands Lladró and Sargadelos can be found in homes across Spain but Gallardo has captured the imagination of a younger audience by rethinking classic motifs and creating elaborate modern designs, reminiscent

"Global fast-fashion chains and high-end brands aside, what surprises a returning visitor such as myself is the deepening diversification of local retail, much of which proudly waves the 'Made in Spain' flag"

Three shops to check out
—
01 Galería Loewe
Browse Loewe's high-quality leather goods.
02 Glent
Head here for bespoke men's shoes.
03 Andrés Gallardo
A mecca for quirky porcelain jewellery.

of classy old-school Spanish jewellery. In other words, expect a significant number of flowers, birds and tree branches in block colours.

Alongside Gallardo is Helena Rohner, who sells her exclusive tableware and porcelain jewellery out of a snug showroom (*see page 52*) on the cobbled Calle del Almendro. Rohner's whimsical tea sets for Georg Jensen have been gracing kitchen tables across Europe since the 1990s, when the Barcelona-born designer first collaborated with the Danish silversmith. Since then she's gained plenty of devoted followers with an appreciation for small-run handmade products.

Rubbing shoulders with Gallardo and Rohner is young Álvaro Ruiz of Guantes Luque (*see page 61*), a glove shop and manufacturer that has been in business since 1896. Beyond the cute canine logo embellished above the entrance, Ruiz – the fourth generation of this family business – purveys hand-cut and hand-stitched gloves that garner the attention of Spanish socialites and European royals, as well as playing a star role in Disney's latest version of *Cinderella*. The tiny atelier has managed to stay afloat despite the country's recent economic turmoil by only producing small batches of the intricate designs – and, to ensure steady sales, never dropping the ball on quality.

Speaking of longlasting traditional businesses, here comes Antigua Casa Crespo (*see page 61*) on the unassuming Calle del Divino Pastor in Malasaña.

Entering this charmingly cluttered espadrilles haven is like stepping back into the past; the venture opened its doors in 1863 and not much seems to have changed since. What started as a shop selling simple sandals for workers now handcrafts and sells espadrilles of various styles and colours, attracting everyone from Spanish *abuelas* waiting to replace their decades-favourite models to overly excited Harajuku girls anxious to get hold of a precious pair.

If you visit you'll get to know the dark wooden façade very well as no doubt you'll be confronted by a tedious queue – but be patient as it's well worth the wait. The average price is €25 per pair and Antigua Casa Crespo also happens to be the only store in Madrid with its own factory. As the latest member of the founding family to take the reins, Maxi Garbayo never misses an opportunity to talk about his production house's humble location in the village of Cervera del Río Alhama. Just remember not to touch the display merchandise if you want to stay on his good side.

The strategy of keeping retail small and in the family seems to be paying off for the likes of Garbayo, Rohner, Ruiz and Gallardo – and soon it might be catching on elsewhere in Spain. The latest economic figures show a continuous rise in retail sales, helping the domestic economy to grow at one of the fastest rates in the EU.

So it seems like good news for the Spanish economy, as well as small family-run shops in the city and ultimately us – the shoppers. Make sure you leave some room in your suitcase on your way here – and pack some comfortable walking shoes. — (M)

ABOUT THE WRITER: Gocheva is the founding editor of The Monocle Travel Guide Series. Having been with MONOCLE since 2009, she also set up the Toronto bureau and has done her fair share of travels around the world. The best part of her job? Scouting her favourite cities for top retail, obviously.

ESSAY 02
Ripe for a refill
Vermouth's revival

─────

For a long time in Madrid, 'vermut' would be ordered solely by elderly gents propping up the bar and reliving their youths. But the fortified wine has made a welcome return – and it's much classier than sangría.

by Paula Móvil, food journalist

If you've just touched down in Madrid you might not yet realise it but vermouth is in the midst of a comeback. For years it was seen as the exclusive drink of the bevy of elderly Spanish men hanging about the old-style bars dotted across the city. However, a new generation of young *Madrileños* has started switching their *cubatas* (tall spirit-based drinks) for a glass of richly flavoured *vermut*. Perhaps it was borne of the need for a lighter drink as they sat on sun-drenched terraces nursing their Sunday hangovers, or maybe it's a natural offshoot of Spain's gastronomical boom and the insatiable search to reinvent old trends. What is clear is that the newfound embrace of this elixir is in full swing. If chefs are the new rock stars, vermouth is the new hit song.

The first thing you'll need to know before you order your own *vermut* is how to pronounce it. A true *Madrileño* drops the "t", affectionately referring to their favourite drink as *vermú*. This fortified wine is flavoured with up to 80 macerated botanicals and is actually one of the most *castizo* (a term for anything that is authentically Spanish) concoctions in the capital. However, the roots of this medicinal wine can be tracked all the way back to India in 1500BC and traces of it were even found inside a Chinese mummy from 1200BC.

Fast forward a few millennia to 1786 and an Italian named Antonio Benedetto Carpano was so inspired by a bitter botanical called *wermut* (German for wormwood) that he created his own label: Carpano Antica Formula. This went on to inspire other concoctions around Europe and in Spain the tradition took hold in Reus in Catalonia with wineries such as Miró, De Muller, Rofes and Yzaguirre. This Spanish offshoot was flavoured with cinnamon instead of the vanilla favoured by the Italians.

The main champions of vermouth are the popular traditional

Vermut hotspots
——
01 El Boquerón, Lavapiés
Rowdy hangout for locals.
02 Bodegas Casas, Atocha
This 'taberna' serves 'vermut'
with a splash of 'sifón'.
**03 Casa Camacho,
Malasaña**
Well-versed drinkers and
young enthusiasts.

bars that have been serving it on tap for generations. For a while though it was an endangered species, following decades of creeping domination from big-name beer and wine. You may also be wondering where sangria fits into this distilled equation. While we love to indulge in a pitcher of the latter while holidaying down by the beach or rampaging at a fiesta at home, the truth is that Spaniards don't drink this fruity mixture as much as the foreign stereotype would have you believe. If you're looking to avoid raising eyebrows as another misled *guiri* (foreigner), approach the bar with confidence, look the bartender in the eye and order a *vermú*.

Almost every 100-year-old *taberna* in the city serves *vermut de grifo* (vermouth on tap) and a sign on the façade is usually a surefire sign of whether a bar is worth your valuable drinking time. One such bar is El Boquerón (Calle Valencia 14), a bastion of tradition within the multicultural Lavapiés district (*see page 130*). You'll only fit in here if you're partial to throwing olive

pits, napkins and prawn heads on the ground as you slurp down some juicy oysters with one hand and sip on the perfect glass of *vermut* with the other. A short walk from Atocha's railway station, Bodegas Casas (Avenida de la Ciudad de Barcelona 23) is another venue that serves the drink to perfection with a splash of *sifón* (soda water) – but only if you manage to successfully fight your way through the army of patrons crowding the steel-surfaced bar.

Many of the older gentlemen at bars such as these can testify to the charming allure of *vermú* in their younger years. In the past, if you wanted to get near a young woman on a Sunday after church, inviting her to drink a glass of *vermut* was the way to do it. Today, as these same men stand at the bar reminiscing about their former womanising ways, they are joined by a younger generation who are watering down *vermut*'s reputation as an old man's drink. A perfect place to witness this is Casa Camacho (Calle de San Andrés 4), which is located right in the middle of the buzzing Malasaña neighbourhood (*see page 128*) and opened in 1928. Dusty bottles line the shelves on the back wall and the traditional *raciones* of food filter out of a

> "*Approach the bar with confidence, look the bartender in the eye and order a 'vermú'*"

questionably grimy kitchen. Yet the bar is always packed due to the quality of their *vermú*. For an extra kick ask for the *yayo*: a dangerous mix of gin, vermouth and soda.

The ideal time to knock back this drink is *la hora del aperitivo* or "the time of the aperitif", which is assigned to the late evening, usually just before one of the city's infamously late dinners. Without running the risk of derailing your appetite, you may want to order the perfect edible accompaniment: a skewered *tapa* or *gilda* made of olives, peppers or anchovies. Remember the movie *Gilda*? Well actress Rita Hayworth was considered to be "spicy and hot" just like the *piparra* (green pepper) on this skewer.

The spirited comeback of vermouth, fuelled by a new enthusiastic generation, has certainly given this liquid a new lease of life in Madrid. Sure, the city is ripe with the newest gastronomic trends and home to a multitude of Michelin-starred restaurants but before you tantalise your palate with these modern morsels, take a moment to embrace the sacred ritual of the aperitivo. Raise your glass to the resilience of this traditional tipple as you toast: "*Viva el vermú!*" — (M)

ABOUT THE WRITER: Móvil is a food journalist from Guatemala who moved to the Spanish capital in 2003. Together with her partner Roberto Castán, she converted her obsession for *vermut* into La Vermutería Pop-up, a mobile bar that springs up at some of the city's (and country's) most popular events.

ESSAY 03
Acquired tastes
Madrid's must-tries

————

Although the Spanish capital is overflowing with global flavours, its local signature dishes – from intestines to testicles – are required eating if you want to experience the culinary scene in all its glory.

by Maria Arranz, editor

Madrid has a reputation for welcoming people from all over the country and being a good host. In fact, a huge chunk of Spain's rural population migrated from the countryside to the capital in the mid-20th century in search of greener urban pastures. This has underwritten the city's love of more humble delicacies but may also explain why residents are so willing to try new flavours.

It explains how in a neighbourhood such as Lavapiés you can still see *manolo* bars (traditional working-class drinking spots) alongside restaurants fragranced by the exotic aromas of curried vegetables prepared by a new wave of south Asian immigrants. The cramped streets are home to more than 80 nationalities and restaurants offer tastes from Africa (Baobab, La Teranga), the UK (Los Chuchis) and Mexico (Antigua Taquería).

At weekends the *calles* of La Latina are a popular stomping ground for *Madrileños* as they peruse the stalls of the famous

El Rastro flea market. But traditional *tabernas* are now wedged between diverse gastronomic proposals such as the Russian specialities of El Cosaco, the Italian and Argentinian recipes of Camoatí and the renowned fusion cuisine of LaCcava, with a menu that mixes French, Mexican, Arabic and American flavours.

However, while it's perfectly understandable that you would want to take your palate on a whirlwind world tour, if you're in Madrid (and you have a strong stomach) you ought to try some of the more extreme and greasy specialities that are unique to the city itself. The flagship dish is the *cocido Madrileño*: a hearty stew made from chickpeas, vegetables and a wide assortment of meats, whose recipe goes back to mediaeval times. Originally a humble dish, its popular reputation saw it travel up the social hierarchy to the tables of kings. Ask anyone where to find the best *cocido* and they will probably point you in the direction of their mother's house. But there are a number of restaurants known for this speciality, such as Lhardy, La Bola and the classic among classics, Malacatín. If you're feeling even more ravenous (and adventurous) try *callos* (tripe stew) and *casquería* (offal), the most authentic of Madrid meals. Thanks to the skills of the city's chefs, people are usually surprised at just how delicious these dishes are in traditional *tabernas* like Maldonado 14, Bodegas Ricla and San Mamés.

"If you're feeling even more ravenous (and adventurous) try 'callos' (tripe stew) and 'casquería' (offal), the most authentic of Madrid meals"

Still feeling bold? Indulge in some succulent *criadillas* (testicles), a star item on the menu of the Chamberí district's Casa Ricardo. Other restaurants, such as the Arganzuela district's Freiduría de Gallinejas, fry up servings of *gallinejas*, *entresijos* and *zarajos* (chicken or lamb intestines).

For those with a sweet tooth, Madrid also has a longstanding tradition of deliciously greasy sweets. *Churros* and *porras* reign from breakfast through to the wee hours, when they are devoured by those stumbling home after a big night. The crunchy batter and dipping chocolate are also popular during the folkloric festivals that pop up in various neighbourhoods during the warmer months. But legendary institution Chocolatería San Ginés, just a few paces from Plaza Mayor, makes them all year round. *Torrijas*, an unlikely dessert made from slices of bread soaked in milk or wine and then fried, is most popular during Easter.

If you're still feeling tentative about sinking your teeth into these treasures, include a trip to the corner bar first. One of the city's skilled *caña*-pouring bartenders will be at the ready to serve you a welcome dose of liquid courage. — (M)

ABOUT THE WRITER: The editor of magazines *Madriz* and *Fuet*, Arranz specialises in gastronomy and food culture. She has left the city in search of greener pastures on numerous occasions – admitting to a love-hate relationship with her home city – but she always comes back.

ESSAY 04
City of two halves
Real vs Atlético

Think of football in the Spanish capital and the first club to spring to mind will be Europe's most successful: Real Madrid. However, that would be to forget Atlético: rivals and a key part of the city's sporting culture.

*by Ben Olsen,
writer*

When getting to grips with a new city, exploring its geography, language, history and current affairs can add a valuable sense of context. Yet in Madrid, football paints an equally valid picture. Here the beautiful game left bullfighting way back in the Ernest Hemingway era as Spain's number-one sport; it has the power to bring the city to a standstill and turn traditionally back-page headlines into front-page news. The colours of its two largest clubs – the white of Real Madrid and striped red and white, or *rojiblanco*, of Atlético Madrid – are emblematic of the city. The clubs' contrasting histories and fortunes play a large part in defining those who live here.

Madrid's footballing heritage is legendary. In the form of Real Madrid, the capital can lay claim to Europe's most successful club – having won more trophies than any other team on the continent – and the world's richest, topping Deloitte's World's Richest Club list for 10 years running. The club's champagne moments have been delivered by a generation-spanning who's who of sporting greats, including Zinedine Zidane, David Beckham and Cristiano Ronaldo.

Propped up by a sophisticated global marketing wing, the club's presence plays a major role in drawing tourists to the city. Yet as fans of the city's second-largest club Atlético Madrid point out, despite a relative lack of success there is more to the story than *Los Blancos*.

The two clubs embody Madrid's turbulent modern history and the socio-economic and political divisions between its people. Both teams, founded within a year of each other at the turn of the 20th century, occupy opposite sides of the city. Real Madrid's Santiago Bernabéu stadium is in the leafy,

Ways to stay fit

01 Cycling
Explore the city on two wheels and complete the Madrid Río cycling lap.
02 Swimming
Try Piscina Municipal El Lago.
03 Running lounge
We've mapped out routes that weave past the sights (*see page 126*).

"The two clubs embody Madrid's turbulent modern history and socio-economic and political divisions"

wealthy northern district of Chamartín, near the major banks and glitzy commerce of the Paseo de la Castellana. Atlético ply their trade at the more modest Vicente Calderón stadium, which is set between a brewery and the choked M30 motorway by the Manzanares River in the unfashionable south.

Historically one of Madrid's poorer neighbourhoods, Arganzuela's working-class population has traditionally shaped the *rojiblanco* fanbase that has lived in the shadows of their illustrious rivals for years. Ever since General Franco piggybacked Real Madrid's dominance in the European game during the 1950s for political capital, the club's association with the regime and the nation's upper echelons has burned bright. Atlético was seen at the time as an outlet for the rebellion: the people versus the power; Robin Hood versus the rich.

Although such lines have since blurred in the bodegas around the capital, badinage between both clubs' fans treads similar lines. The phrase *Atléti hasta la muerte, Real hasta la próxima derrota* (Atléti till I die, Real until the next defeat) reflects the perceived difference between those through-thick-and-

thin fans who stand by Atlético – season-ticket sales famously went up when the team were relegated to the second tier – and Real Madrid's hobbyist fans who'll only sing when they're winning. Yet ask a Real fan and they'll likely laugh this off, point towards the club's monumental success and possibly bring up the old *"Patético* Atlético" insult. Playing on the *rojiblancos* lack of success, a famous advertisement from 2006 once saw a young boy ask his father why they support Atlético; his father struggles to find a response.

For all their differences, Real and Atlético are key parts of the city's beating heart. Keeping an industry of cleaners in jobs sweeping up the discarded husks of *pipas* – the salted sunflower seeds eaten in bulk in both stadiums – the sport is part of *Madrileños'* shared identity. A hotly contested annual event sees runners of both stripes race between the Bernabéu and Calderón stadiums. Matchdays transform the city into colourful pageants, fans toting *bocadillos de jamón* and Mahou beer as they flock from Nuevos Ministerios Metro in the north and Pirámides in the south towards their respective grounds.

Plaza de Cibeles has been adopted by Real Madrid's fans as a site of celebration, trophy wins seeing tens of thousands descend on the square and the team's flag draped over the statue. When Atlético triumph it's the nearby Neptune Fountain that gushes red and white. Yet, as the club's fans are more than aware, these occasions are far rarer.

It's when the two teams meet head to head in *El Derbi Madrileño* that visitors witness the sport's full effect on the city. The world's highest-profile club competition – the European Champions League – saw the teams meet in the 2014 final and although the game was played in Lisbon, the build-up in Madrid was deafening. Allegiances were displayed across the city and giant replica shirts draped in Puerta del Sol. Despite taking the lead in the first half, Atlético conceded an equaliser after 93 minutes before Real won the game 4-1 in extra time, securing *la décima*: a record-breaking 10th Champions League victory. Half of the city rejoiced with a two-day party soundtracked by a cacophony of car horns. Real ruled the capital once more – though Atlético fans had the solace of first place in that season's domestic league, having finished three points ahead of their city rivals.

So 2014 was just another chapter in the city's sporting drama. In victory and defeat, it's the perennial hopes, near misses and euphoric triumphs that embellish the cultural dividing line that defines Madrid's passionate people. — (M)

ABOUT THE WRITER: Previously MONOCLE's senior sub editor, Olsen is now a freelance writer. This naturally gives him more flexibility when it comes to attending important football games, be they in Spain or his homeland of England.

ESSAY 05

Reel Madrid
The city on screen

Pedro Almodóvar, Spain's most famous director, brought the capital to the film world's attention by making it the star of numerous outings. Since then it has played host to everyone from Jason Bourne to the Antichrist.

by David Bernal, film critic

In one of Pedro Almodóvar's first films, *Labyrinth of Passion* (1982), the son of an emperor travels to Madrid and declares it "the most fun city in the world". He wasn't wrong. At the time the city was experiencing an explosion of creativity in the post-Franco era, known as *La Movida Madrileña*. The countercultural movement was a catharsis that marked the transition from old Madrid to the Madrid of today. But many of the older rituals in the film have not been lost: waking early on a Sunday for El Rastro (a flea market in the old La Latina quarter that dates back to 1740) then snacking on a calamari sandwich at one of the *tabernas*.

Almodóvar is the director who has best portrayed Madrid's soul on film and his work cannot be understood without taking into account the city's influence. In his films Madrid is always a main character, sharing the big screen with the likes of Penélope Cruz, Antonio Banderas, Carmen Maura and Victoria Abril. The drama *What Have*

I Done to Deserve This? (1984) was set in one of the working-class *colmena* residences, while comedy *Women on the Verge of a Nervous Breakdown* (1988) was shot in a penthouse. Both films star Carmen Maura but while the first is a neorealist depiction of the city, the second opts for modern imagery. So which is more accurate? Well, both. Madrid is a city of contrasts where everyone mixes together. At a party you may rub shoulders with a duchess and a drag queen. This is its charm.

The filmography of *el Manchego*, as Almodóvar is known, serves as a guide to some of the city's most beautiful corners. Characters from *The Flower of My Secret* (1996) dance under the stars in a deserted Plaza Mayor. The nurse in *Talk to Her* (2002) watches silent films in the Cine Doré on Calle de Santa Isabel 3, a cinema that houses the Spanish film archive.

Almodóvar isn't the only one to use Madrid as a film set. Film-makers of the 1990s no longer saw the city as a capital dominated by a dictator; instead they painted a cosmopolitan metropolis. These new films broke with tradition and embraced Hollywood genres.

In *The Day of the Beast*, (1995), director Álex de la Iglesia set the arrival of the Antichrist atop the Torres Kio, a pair of skyscrapers in the financial district. The premise had some justification: Madrid is one of the only cities with a monument to Lucifer, standing tall in Retiro Park. Iglesia's picture includes one of the most iconic images in Spanish film: a priest and a metalhead hanging from the Schweppes sign crowning the Gran Vía skyline.

Two years later Alejandro Amenábar, Spain's highest-grossing director, emptied the city's busiest boulevard to film a sequence in his thriller *Open Your Eyes* (1997). Tom Cruise tried to emulate the scene in Times Square but his 2001 remake *Vanilla Sky* lacked one key element: Madrid.

> *"Film-makers of the 1990s no longer saw the city as a capital dominated by a dictator; instead they painted a cosmopolitan metropolis"*

Despite the city's modernity, a pure Madrid still exists. This Madrid *castizo* is caricatured in the *Torrente* saga, whose five instalments star comedian Santiago Segura as the antihero: a scumbag cop and Atlético fan who struts the ungentrified streets and frequents bars with floors covered in prawn tails. American and French producers bought the rights for a remake but such characters are usually lost in translation.

Obviously Madrid hasn't gone unnoticed in Hollywood. *The Bourne Ultimatum* (2007), for example, includes scenes in Atocha's railway station and alongside the iconic Viaducto de la Calle Bailén. But the film-maker who perhaps best took Madrid's pulse was Jim Jarmusch. *The Limits of Control* (2009) shows the space-age architecture of the Torres Blancas residence near Avenida de América and actress Tilda Swinton meeting assassin Isaach De Bankolé in Plaza de San Ildefonso, Malasaña. As it happens, this bohemian neighbourhood is the perfect place to drink *cañas* and gather evidence for Madrid, quite possibly, being the most fun city in the world. — (M)

ABOUT THE WRITER: Madrid-born film-buff Bernal has shared his film knowledge in *Cinemania, Rolling Stone* and *El País* and reviewed films on radio station Cadena SER and cable TV station Canal+. His favourite Madrid film is *The Day of the Beast.*

Madrid's movies

01 Almodóvar's oeuvre
The city is the backdrop for most of his pictures.
02 The Day of the Beast
Taking its premise from the notorious monument of Lucifer.
03 Open Your Eyes
Madrid's busiest boulevard was emptied for this film.

ESSAY 06
Modern makeover
Reshaping the city

―――

Charming relics still remain here and there on Madrid's streets but an energetic new generation is taking the lead on urban renewal. This heady mix of old and new makes for an all-singing – and all-inclusive – city.

by Liam Aldous,
Monocle

Shaped by centuries of conservative royal rule and a stifling 40-year fascist dictatorship, Madrid is derided by most Spaniards as an old-fashioned cloister for the country's political and economic elite. It's too *casposo* they say, screwing up their faces as if being forced to chew on some bitter *jamón*.

For those of you who are unfamiliar with the joys of Spanish jargon, the literal translation of *casposo* is "dandruffy". The term is usually applied to disparage "old Spain" and conjures up the image of an elderly *señor* with a stiff upper lip, his hair slicked back with Brylcreem and shoulders speckled with flakes of dandruff. Deeply ingrained perceptions are hard to

shake and even though Madrid has undergone a modern makeover, much of the country still regards the capital with dandruff-laden disdain.

But if you're travelling to Madrid (or are already here) pay no attention to the naysayers. Today it is barely recognisable from the stuffy city of old. The most visible tokens of change have been the big-ticket infrastructure projects such as Madrid Río (*see page 111*) and the relocation of city hall to the Palacio de Cibeles. However, a protracted economic crisis and political malaise have seen other massive projects grind to a halt, prompting residents to step into roles as reformers and spur change on a smaller scale.

The explosion of entrepreneurial energy continues to reverberate across each boisterous *barrio* and down nearly every colourful *calle*. In Las Salesas an old bread factory has been converted into organic food market and restaurant El Huerto de Lucas (*see page 46*); a former newspaper's HQ is now El Imparcial (Calle Duque de Alba 4), a smart restaurant with an

Top three revivals

01 Matadero Madrid
This cultural precinct is not to be missed (see page 98).
02 San Antón Church
The pews have been given a hi-tech upgrade.
03 El Huerto de Lucas
An organic food market that you could potentially spend all day in.

"Proud business owners and grateful residents are spearheading a more sustainable city facelift" editorially themed gift-shop; while a hollowed-out cinema has been remade into multi-level fitness centre Gymage (*see page 122*). As privately financed dreams have become a reality, proud business owners and grateful residents are spearheading a more sustainable city facelift.

Nowhere is this metamorphosis more evident than in the rebadged Ballesta Triangle. Tucked away behind Gran Vía, these streets fell into disrepair following Spain's economic crisis in the 1990s, becoming sullied by crime, drugs and debauchery. In 2007 a private investment group purchased the dozens of brothels smothering the streets, renovating each premise and intentionally lowering rents to attract creatively inclined tenants. In the years since, the turnaround has seen independent retailers such as Kikekeller (Calle Corredera Baja de San Pablo 17) move in to sell a range of metallic furniture (and transform its space into a bar at night), while a former butcher has become the Microteatro (Calle de Loreto Prado y Enrique Chicote 9): a miniature theatre complex for acting, writing and directing talent.

Yet as moribund spaces have been snapped up, stripped back and reborn, many of the vestiges of a different era still litter the streets. A whistle worthy of the Pied Piper heralds the arrival of a gypsy knife-sharpener who regularly wheels his cart around the city in the evenings. *Serenos* – a dying breed of night watchmen – still patrol certain streets in Chamberí; a dogged museum continues to attract fans of *tauromaquia* in the Las Ventas bullfighting ring; and legions of pilgrims do some serious heavy-lifting as they prepare for Semana Santa (Holy Week). This daily juxtaposition between old and new further stirs up the city's chaotic feel but it also grounds the capital in authenticity.

As a new generation of spirited citizenry begins to eclipse the old guard, the city's resilient character has also given rise to some bizarre quirks. For example, the Church of San Antón in the Chueca district, best known for its annual blessing of animals, recently went hi-tech: it installed television screens with a live feed to the Vatican, free wi-fi, smartphone-charging points and a confessional iPad app, available 24/7.

In addition, those looking to satisfy their sweet tooth can visit young entrepreneur Isabel Ottino, who has opened small repository El Jardín del Convento (Calle del Cordón 1) near Plaza Mayor, which sells traditional cakes and confectionery from convents around the country. Over in Malasaña, a traditional delicatessen has even installed a street-side vending machine that dispenses neatly packaged *jamón ibérico*, manchego cheese and tortilla.

But the city's rebirth is not merely cosmetic. Madrid is more tolerant and liberal than ever; waves of immigrants have added progressive flavour to its menus and culture. The city's gay pride festival draws about two million people onto the streets in a celebration of diversity and, in 2015, new 71-year-old mayor Manuela Carmena stood before crowds to proclaim the "importance of sexuality and sensuality in the quest for individual and social happiness". The contrast with leaders of old was astonishing, the applause deafening.

So what of that rancid, recalcitrant, dandruff-speckled man who once personified Madrid? He may be less ubiquitous than ever but if you look hard enough you might still spot these walking relics inside the unchanged drinking holes of Barrio Salamanca or Chamberí. Some hug the bar, sipping on *cañas* as they grumble about Madrid's loss of innocence. However in true *Madrileño* form, most simply shrug their shoulders, acquiescing to the inevitable march of change that has been ushered in by a more determined generation. What a difference a decade makes. — (M)

ABOUT THE WRITER: MONOCLE's man in Madrid moved to Spain from Australia in 2011. Between his assignments for us he has worked as everything from teacher to tourism blogger and even scored a (fleeting) role on one of Spain's popular TV shows: *El Intermedio*.

ESSAY 07
Facing Franco
Putting history to bed
———

Four decades after the death of Francisco Franco, the legacy of Spain's dictator can still be felt in Madrid's streets and buildings. Plans are afoot to change that – but still no one can decide what to do with his mausoleum.

by Pablo León, writer

Spain's dictator Francisco Franco died on 20 November 1975 after 40 years in power. The country has now been a democracy for as long as it was stifled by his authoritarian regime. Madrid, the capital city, the cosmopolitan apple of the country's eye, the effervescent epicentre of all things cultural, was also Franco's city. The elite of El Caudillo (or The Leader) would sashay along its roads; they were mayors, ministers and industrialists and Madrid's avenues were soon named after them. Entire neighbourhoods, such as Salamanca, became hubs for Francoist ideology.

Since then we've had the Transición: the process by which Spain evolved into a democracy, completed by the approval of its current constitution in 1978. Then there was the 2007 law under the then prime minister José Luis Rodríguez Zapatero, which condemned Franco's regime and sought to right the wrongs of that era. Yet still El Caudillo hasn't left the

Spanish capital completely. You can still walk the Calle de los Caídos de la División Azul, a street that is dedicated to the Fallen of the Blue Division, a detachment sent by Franco to help the Nazis during the Second World War. In the city's north you can also visit Nuevos Ministerios, a gargantuan ministerial building that resembles an edifice from Hitler's Berlin.

"Let's go walk in the city centre; we'll get off at the Gran Vía Metro stop and we can walk from there," I say to my 82-year-old grandmother. "That was José Antonio's stop," she replies automatically. She is one of the last of her generation to remember Madrid's turbulent history first-hand. She goes on to tell me how Gran Vía, Madrid's iconic main street, was officially inaugurated by King Alfonso XIII on 4 April 1910. But Franco later changed its name to honour José Antonio Primo de Rivera, the commander behind one of Spain's biggest coups d'état (there have been quite a few) and a leader of the Falange, the political organisation behind Spanish fascism.

At the end of this sumptuous retail strip sits Plaza de España, a typically *Madrileño* square dominated by two buildings: the iconic neo-baroque Edificio España and the 37-floor-high Torre de Madrid. Both were designed by Spanish architects Julián and José María Otamendi Machimbarrena as an assignment of the Metropolitan Real Estate Agency to symbolise the prosperity of Franco's Spain. Work on the former started during the dictatorship's heyday in

"Franco's mausoleum is open for tourists and attracts quite the crowd. It receives more than 200,000 visitors each year, who are drawn there either by morbid curiosity or a respect for history"

> **Three buildings from Franco's era**
>
> **01 Edificio España**
> This neo-baroque building is an imposing landmark.
> **02 Torre de Madrid**
> Get a great view of the city.
> **03 Nuevos Ministerios**
> Sprawling cement ministry in the financial district.

1948. The design was intended to follow that of the Chicago School: to build a towering skyscraper and attract the world's attention. It was inaugurated on 4 October 1953 and lauded by the press. "Our city's standing as one of the great European capitals is elevated by the luxurious Plaza Hotel in the superb Edificio España, the pride and joy of this new and grand Madrid," said the *ABC* paper, as it sang the praises of El Caudillo's city.

The reach of Franco's legacy extends to the outskirts of the Spanish capital. The first thing a visitor will notice in the nearby Cuelgamuros Valley is the imposing Cruz de los Caídos ("The Cross of the Fallen") on top of the Valle de los Caídos basilica. It was inaugurated on 1 April 1959, two decades after the Day of Victory that ended the Civil War and marked the beginning of the Franco era.

The dictator himself was at the unveiling of the memorial. "I sang for him – I sang for Franco," says Ángel de la Torrent, an 80-year-old parish priest whose connection to the cross is almost a lifelong affair. More than 30,000 of the soldiers who fell in the Civil War are buried there. And in November 1975, they were joined by Franco himself. His corpse still lies there today.

Franco's mausoleum is open for tourists and attracts quite the crowd. It receives more than 200,000 visitors each year, who are drawn either by morbid curiosity or a respect for history. As a historical monument it could be so much more and a number of people would argue that there is a conspicuous absence of information about the Civil War and the dictator himself. Even four decades after the end of Francoism, the country still can't come to an agreement on how to treat this controversial valley. "It's a hot potato for any government no matter what their ideology is," says Pablo Linares, president of the Association in Defense of the Valley.

After 40 years of democracy the shadow of the imperial eagle seen in Franco's version of the Spanish flag has continued to glide over Madrid. However, change is in the air. A new political party took the reins of the city council in June 2015 and has promised to rethink the destiny of the remaining Franco-era street signs.

Such a move is certain to stir the ghosts of Spain's recent past but mayor Manuela Carmena believes it will also help Madrid's inhabitants to reimagine these contentious parts of the city map through an open, inclusive debate. Locals will finally have their say on who they think deserves to be honoured by the city and see the names of some more inclusive figures emblazoned on the capital's *calles*. — (M)

ℹ️

ABOUT THE WRITER: León has been covering culture, travel, history and politics for Spanish daily *El País* since 2009. An avid cyclist and proud fourth-generation *Madrileño* (which makes him a *gato*), the young writer can often be spotted around the city having a beer with his sprightly grandmother.

ESSAY 08

Winning isn't everything
Olympic optimism

Madrid has fallen at the last hurdle on three bids for the Games. Yet a legacy is apparent regardless: improved infrastructure and an impressive public-transport network. Has triumph emerged from adversity?

by Luis Mendoza, Monocle

Ever since Barcelona hosted the 1992 Olympics, Madrid has tried to mirror the deed in an attempt to gain international recognition and attract the flocks of tourists that come with it. You can't accuse the city of lacking tenacity: its first unsuccessful bid was back in 1972 when General Franco was still in power.

However, the real push has been over the past decade as the city has flexed its administrative muscles, determined to devise a winning bid. It tried to secure the 2012 games but lost out to London, then narrowly succumbed to Rio de Janeiro for the 2016 event and most recently were deprived of the 2020 Games which, despite high hopes, were awarded to Tokyo.

This stubbornness is understandable. In Spain the 1992 Barcelona games are seen as a coming-of-age moment for an old-fashioned nation, still viewed as the turning point in a long journey to becoming a modern democracy. As a city Barcelona continues to revel in its Olympic legacy, which endures as an exemplary model of transformation and regeneration. The sporting event remade the Mediterranean city from an industrial backwater into a cosmopolitan seaside metropolis. It was a boost for jobs, infrastructure and tourism; Barcelona is now the 10th most visited city in Europe, luring more than seven million visitors a year (Madrid currently attracts four-and-a-half million).

Add the infamous Madrid-Barcelona rivalry to the mix and it's no wonder the capital has been trying to bask in some of its own Olympic glow. Nonetheless, consistent failure across three consecutive bids has prompted a mild inferiority complex – and disparaging comments from their proud Catalan compatriots certainly haven't alleviated the pain.

That said, once you cut through the politics you can see just how much the city has already benefited from these failed attempts. It begs the question: who needs the headache of hosting the world's biggest sporting event if the city has already been transformed? Successive bids have improved the city's transport infrastructure as well as cultural and sport facilities. A number of stadiums were built (although perhaps one too many) and the city now enjoys an ample network of modern venues to host international competitions, big conferences and festivals for music and the arts. A good example is the Caja Mágica, an impressive cubic structure with retractable roofs that

"Who needs the headache of hosting the world's biggest sporting event if the city has already been transformed?"

can accommodate important tennis and basketball tournaments as well as concerts.

Another grand project is Madrid Río (*see page 111*). The park is probably the capital's most ambitious and far-reaching redevelopment to date, having buried the city's main ring road that used to run along the Manzanares River and split the city in two. The ambitious plan returned plenty of public space to *Madrileños* in the form of a vast riverside green playground with additional sport facilities that are open to the public. It also included the redevelopment of Matadero Madrid (*see page 98*), an old abattoir in the Arganzuela district that quickly established itself as the premiere cultural precinct with large venues accommodating various art exhibitions, theatre festivals and music gigs.

Moving around the city on public transport is also much easier thanks to Madrid's seemingly endless pursuit of the Olympic dream. Today, the Metro is lauded as one of Europe's most comprehensive and efficient networks. Many new lines have been built to reach the city's outskirts, allowing more people to get to work using the underground and making the city less car dependent in the process. In recent years city hall has been trying to encourage urban cycling too, launching public bicycle scheme BiciMad in 2014. It was especially good news for a city so commonly scourged by painful traffic jams.

Of course many of these Olympic-fuelled improvements have come at a hefty cost. Quite a few residents would say that while infrastructure redevelopments were indeed timely and necessary for the capital, many of the new imposing stadiums have

Key stations

01 Nuevos Ministerios
Get your airport-bound train from this station.
02 Ópera
Host to an underground archaeological museum.
03 Atocha
The city's first railway station is a must-visit.

burdened the city with unnecessary debt. A subsequent financial crisis has seen the desire to host the Games waver and a weary public now believes that perhaps it's about time to take our hat out of the Olympic ring altogether.

The previous bids have helped the city learn some valuable lessons. In 2013, when former mayor Ana Botella took to the podium to tout Madrid's virtues in a final speech for the 2020 bid, her cringe-worthy English was universally ridiculed at home and abroad. While many *Madrileños* responded to the embarrassing speech with humour (signs sprung up around the city offering one of the mayor's *café con leche*, to which she jarringly made reference), it was a searing reminder that Spaniards need to work harder on their English skills if they want to welcome a more international crowd.

The growth of our transport network has also highlighted how important urban mobility is to the city's changing fortunes as a financial capital. The bids may have been put on hold for now but no one thinks local authorities should drop the ball on a proud public-transport network.

Most importantly there has been a more practical shift in priorities. Instead of chasing the elusive games, the city has started to look closer to home and is investing in a new generation of young *Madrileños* instead. After all, these homegrown entrepreneurs are the modern-day athletes most likely to deliver the city onto the podium of prosperity. — (M)

ABOUT THE WRITER: Madrid-native Luis Mendoza is MONOCLE's creative solutions executive. Mendoza moved to London four years ago but returns home regularly as he can't keep away from his favourite Spanish delights: *jamón* and his mother's *croquetas*.

ESSAY 09
Nocturnal adventures
Madrid's nightlife

——

If you want to discover the essence of this city – whether you're planning a crucial business meeting or a relaxed drink with the locals – wait until the sun sets. It's after dark that Madrid truly comes alive.

by Rodrigo Taramona, blogger

The second the sun disappears below the Sierra de Madrid mountains in the west, the city gets noisier, sexier and truer to itself. The night isn't only a time for leisure. Any kind of social interaction, even if strictly professional, is best undertaken once dusk sets in.

The capital's signature approach is to discuss business at lunch, after work or, even better, over dinner. It could be at a crowded bar in Malasaña, the city's coolest quarter; a fancy restaurant on Calle Ponzano, which has the city's best ratio of food fodder; or at one of the many old-fashioned cafeterías on every corner.

Late-night culture runs deep in Madrid's DNA. The infamous – and thankfully unsuccessful – 1981 military coup organised by Lieutenant-Colonel Antonio Tejero was planned in a cafetería called Galaxia (now the Van Gogh Café) on Calle Isaac Peral. The perpetrators named their secret mission after the bar where it all started: "Operación Galaxia".

During countercultural movement La Movida Madrileña in the 1980s, there was a generation that had missed the golden age of Madrid's iconic cocktail bar Museo Chicote (Gran Via 12), where figures such as writer Ernest Hemingway, actress Ava Gardner and bullfighter Manolete spent their wildest days. As such they had to be inventive in finding a suitably unruly drinking hole. Already writing the blueprint for Madrid's modern subculture, the city's young cultural elite were dismayed when the bars and *discotecas* closed each morning at 05.00. This is when *el tanatorio de la M30*, the city's mortuary on Madrid's famous M30 ring road, became the new late-night hangout for artists and streetwise "cats" (this is what natives call each other: *gatos*) to drink the night and morning away.

Picture the scene: distraught families and friends, grieving for their loved ones, confronted by large groups of heavily inebriated late-night revellers. This clash often produced the unlikeliest of conversations: people coming together to chat about the fleeting nature of life, for example. Such profound thoughts are often replicated across town; *Madrileños* have a tendency to want to *arreglar el mundo* ("fix the world") when drink is involved.

"Fly solo around the city on any night of the week and odds are you'll meet someone and end up partying together"

As you stroll around the city you may notice that the people here like to talk a lot. No matter where you're from or what language you speak, someone will gladly chat your ear off. Fly solo around the city on any night of the week and odds are you'll meet someone and end up partying together. If you're still sceptical, pay a visit to Plaza de San Ildefonso in the Malasaña district, where La Bicicleta (*see page 41*) is a melting pot: locals and tourists gather from early morning all the way through the night.

Late-night hangouts

01 Van Gogh Café
Northern neighbourhood favourite on Calle Isaac Peral.
02 Museo Chicote
Longest-standing cocktail bar in Madrid still exuding old-school charm.
03 1862 Dry Bar
Sip on some of Malasaña's best cocktails.

When its doors shut, walk downhill to The Passenger (*see page 43*) or the nearby 1862 Dry Bar (*see page 41*) to sip on some of the neighbourhood's best cocktails.

Fast forward to the break of dawn and you might find yourself having a beer for breakfast – along with a dish of delicious bacon and eggs – at Bar Iberia (Glorieta de Ruiz Jiménez 4), renowned for its unusually early opening time (06.00 is extremely early for a late-sleeping city such as this), making it a favourite pit stop for taxi drivers and night owls.

Madrid's wild behaviour is hard to put into words but an old saying has become the unofficial city slogan: *de Madrid al cielo, y en el cielo un agujero para verlo* ("From Madrid to the skies, and from the skies [we'd want] a small hole to see Madrid"). The phrase, coined by playwright Luis Quiñones de Benavente in the 1600s, resonates because wherever *Madrileños* end up, they continue to look fondly on their colourful, chaotic and nocturnally inclined city. And if this long-distance pang of nostalgia involves more than a couple of them you can bet there will be plenty of empty bottles on the table as they sit around putting the world to rights. — (M)

ABOUT THE WRITER: Former teenage actor, co-owner of The Passenger bar and social-issues blogger for *glamour.es*, Taramona also moonlights as a DJ. He spends his remaining time mending the damage wreaked by his sociopathic yet nonetheless charismatic beagle.

ESSAY 10
Alfresco alliances
Outside space
—

With its perpetual sunshine, open-air terraces and welcoming plazas, Madrid is a city that lives for the outdoors. Join us for a leisurely stroll down some sociable streets.

by Marcus Hurst, editor

Populated by immigrants from across Spain and Latin America, people have long taken to Madrid's streets in search of opportunities. They've mingled among market stalls and in the plazas to meet people, find work and build new lives.

From the 17th century many newcomers to the city settled in *corralas*: cramped buildings held up by wooden pillars, with interior patios and no running water. Often up to eight people were crammed into a space of just 20 sq m so these living quarters were exclusively for washing and sleeping. To have any semblance of a life, time spent in public spaces was an absolute necessity.

The weather helped and still does: annual rainfall barely hits 60 days a year so Madrid's open-air terraces and parks are busy year round. Age is no barrier so as night falls it's not uncommon to see a septuagenarian sandwiched between young revellers drinking at a crowded bar or picking their way through a packed plaza.

The real turning point for this love of inhabiting the streets came during La Movida, the countercultural movement in the 1980s that made Madrid the place for hedonism. Film-maker Pedro Almodóvar is the most famous son of this post-Franco renaissance, a time of earth-shattering cultural change that irrevocably changed the city. The Spanish youth, who during the previous four decades of Franco's dictatorship had been told that everything was a sin, helped elect Enrique Tierno Galván, a 60-year-old university professor, as mayor. Despite his formal attire, he was anything but conservative and embraced the unbridled spirit of La Movida. At a rock concert in 1984 he took to the stage to belt out the infamous words: "*El que no esté colocado, que se coloque!*" ("Whoever's not high yet, get high!"). With Franco repression still fresh in the memory it was a watershed moment.

The mayor continued to encourage people to let loose by bringing back fiestas and street concerts. It wasn't uncommon to find Galván himself having a shot of absinthe in a bar or a cocktail on a pavement terrace. On weekends more than half a million people would fill the *calles*; the city soon became synonymous with fun and debauchery.

"On weekends, more than half a million people would fill the 'calles'; the city soon became synonymous with fun and debauchery"

Leafing through the history books, this penchant for the outdoors is further apparent. Until the early 20th century, most residents did their shopping on the streets, with stalls lining major thoroughfares and squares. Shops used the inside part of their premises to store their products, conducting their business on counters sitting along the front windows. One could buy milk that had only just been extracted from its source, contentedly lowing behind the scenes.

ESSAY 11

Dawn till dusk
The city's bar scene

If you're in Madrid with a thirst it won't take long to quench it; in fact, the choice of venues can be bewildering. You won't go too far wrong wandering into the first place you see; failing that, we've picked out some favourites.

by Pablo Bautista, engineer

In recent years, local authorities have extended terrace licences to 365 days a year to raise tax revenues. The pavements and plazas are more crowded than ever, prompting a citywide debate about the private domination of public space (one of the upsides is being able to drink in a square without the threat of a hefty fine). Fortunately there are still plenty of out-of-the-way places that get the balance right. The expanse of La Latina's Plaza de la Paja has several quality restaurants to choose from; the historic Plaza del Alamillo is only a short walk away; and the Plaza de Guardias de Corps in Conde Duque is a pint-sized meeting spot for neighbours.

Prosperity may have reined in the city's wild spirit and banished the cows back to the fields but *Madrileños* are still zealous conquerors of the outdoors. People come to the city to work but they're also drawn in by its fun. If you're a newcomer you'll often find yourself being welcomed by people who, not long ago, were also fresh arrivals. In the public domain everyone is seen as equal and these empathetic *Madrileños* will look you in the eye and make you feel included. You may never see them again but on a warm Madrid night, friendships form easily. It's the city's enduring legacy – and a source of pride. — (M)

ABOUT THE WRITER: Hurst is co-founder of *Yorokobu Magazine*, a Spanish-language monthly publication and blog that covers design, creativity and great ideas based in Madrid. He arrived in the city from the UK 10 years ago and has never looked back.

In 1980 an article published in a Madrid weekly suggested that between the Atocha roundabout and Antón Martín Square – a stretch of barely 700 metres – there were "more bars than in all of Norway". I can't vouch for the importance that other world capitals attach to their bars but in Madrid it's a longstanding tradition to count them.

In the 19th century the writer and city chronicler Ramón de Mesonero Romanos wrote "every building houses a taberna and some even have more than two". In the 1600s a popular song boasted that the city had "300 *tabernas* old and new but only one bookshop". This numbers game endures but while it's fun to count, let me offer some more practical advice.

If you are yet to set foot on Madrid's bustling streets, you may still be hanging on to a few misguided, preconceived ideas about the bar culture. The innards of each Spanish bar often contain large wooden, steel or marble *barras* but the service they provide, the diversity of patrons and the long opening hours make these establishments more than just simple watering holes.

From the early morning hours, *churros* (a deep-fried dough pastry) and *porras* (larger, thicker *churros*) begin flowing over the counter as a sweet and speedy breakfast, while more people appear at around 10.30 for their *café de la mañana*: a sacred morning tea or coffee break that is even stipulated in some workplace agreements and popular among public servants.

Eyes are glued to the TV as people watch the *telediario* news broadcast, cheer as their favourite team scores a goal or scan the endless stream of celebrity gossip programmes, known as the *crónica rosa*, which are favoured by a more elderly audience. Having whirred into life at 07.00, these bars don't roll down their shutters until 02.00. No other type of Spanish business stays open for so long – and they are everywhere.

So where to start? Before asking for tips, explore the streets around your hotel, entering the first one that catches your eye. Leave your

Bars to frequent
—
01 Stop Madrid
A stalwart on Madrid's bar scene – don't be alarmed by the littered floors.
02 Taberna Ángel Sierra
More highbrow but stick to beer, wine and 'vermut'.
03 El Doble
Quench your thirst with a double draft beer.

prejudices at the door: appearances can be deceiving. One foolproof sign is to see how busy the bar is just before lunch or dinner (lunch usually starts around 14.30 and dinner is not earlier than 21.00). You should choose the most crowded. If you can barely make it through the door you're in the right place.

Once inside head straight for the counter; if it's made of marble or stainless steel you might have just stumbled upon a Madrid landmark such as Stop Madrid (on Calle Hortaleza 11) or Cervecería Cervantes (Plaza de Jesús 7). Don't be alarmed by all the shrapnel on the ground: most residents still have the bad habit of throwing their napkins and leftovers on the floor – and proprietors tend to use their brooms sparingly.

If you're inside a classic establishment such as Taberna Ángel Sierra (Calle Gravina 11) and ask for anything other than a beer, wine or vermouth, don't be alarmed if heads turn: people rarely order outside of this holy trinity. For centuries wine reigned supreme in Madrid's bars but in recent decades beer has begun taking its place. Small bottles called *botellines* are popular but if you want to feel like a true Madrileño order a well-poured *caña*. It is just under half a pint of lager, served from a keg at the right pressure with at least half an inch of froth. Ritual demands that the glass be left for a few seconds on the counter and tapped by the waiter. Bars that don't serve well-drawn beer are liable to go broke in under a month so it's serious business. If a small beer won't quench your thirst, double up by ordering *un doble*. Better yet, pay a visit to El Doble (Calle Ponzano 58), which is said to pour the city's best.

"You should choose the most crowded bar. If you can barely make it through the door you're in the right place"

Don't be surprised if your drink is accompanied by a complimentary *tapa*. These popular morsels originated when barmen would cover (or in Spanish "*tapar*") wine glasses with small slices of bread topped with a piece of cold meat in order to prevent flies getting into patrons' drinks. While flies aren't much of a problem these days, many bars in the city still continue the tradition (although not to the competitive extent of their peers in Granada, Salamanca or León). In bars such as Casa Curro (Calle Cava Baja 23) this timeless tradition attracts all sorts of customers, from friends partaking in the jolly custom of *ir de cañas* (bar-hopping) to colleagues gathering for a small *ración* of delicious *gambas*. All of them can be seen sharing delicious tidbits, devouring them with forks, toothpicks or fingers.

The food selection entombed inside the glass casing atop each bar can often be bewildering. You may recognise the *ensaladilla rusa* (potato salad) but choosing from the rest is often a question of pot luck. Avert risk and try Bar Fide's smoked sardines – at one of its outposts on Calle Ponzano 8 or Bretón de los Herreros 17 – the tomato steak at Celso y Manolo (Calle Libertad 1) or the soft-shell crab at Juana La Loca (*see page 34*).

There's a strong chance that, between all the beers and new-found friends, your list of museums and monuments becomes secondary or just ends up trampled among the napkins on the ground. You're advised to view this as an opportunity: missing out on the Prado will provide a perfectly reasonable excuse to come back for a second trip – and another round. — (M)

ABOUT THE WRITER: Bautista lives in the Chamberí district. After helping to redesign Madrid's tourism brand from within the city council, he went on to co-found strategic marketing company Idonika and co-ordinates urban trends festival Mulafest.

ESSAY 12

Cultural pursuit
The Prado

A trip to the capital resulted in Monocle's editor making a last-minute dash to stand in awe of a masterpiece in one of the world's finest galleries. He recommends you do the same – and sample the gin.

by Andrew Tuck,
Monocle

Cultural highlights

01 CentroCentro
A rare glimpse into the city's marbled history.
02 Museo Sorolla
An adventure into the heart of Spanish impressionist painter Jaoquin Sorolla.
03 Galería Helga de Alvear
Europe's biggest private collection.

It's a Thursday morning after a fun – and late-running – Wednesday night. Breakfast has been devoured, several *cortados* supped to find some vigour and we are back on track. Our colleagues have vanished but MONOCLE's Culture editor Robert Bound and I have a couple of hours to kill before take-off. We could crack open our laptops, pretend to read *El País* or perhaps... is there time? Watches are checked. If we left now? Don't dawdle – let's do it.

We jump out into the sunshine of Gran Vía, hail the first cab we see and tell the driver to hit the gas, *por favor*. We want to be the first in the queue when the doors open. We arrive and join a small cluster of people waiting for someone to unlock the doors to the Prado, one of the world's greatest collections of paintings and certainly the finest gathering of Spanish artworks. But while some are waiting to see national treasures such as El Greco's "Nobleman with his Hand on his Chest", whose long face stares at us from his high-pitched ruff,

or Francisco Goya's "The Third of May 1808", depicting Napoleon's troops exacting revenge on Spanish rebels, we are here for a more northerly piece of art exposure.

Tickets are bought and a floorplan secured. If we move fast we will be in front of our quarry within five minutes. We ignore the thousands of faces trying to catch our eyes from behind veils of fissured varnish, turn the corner and there it is: Hieronymous Bosch's "Garden of Earthly Delights", a triptych that takes you from heaven to hell (no, that's not a reference to our Wednesday night). All sorts of sin and lust are depicted and you can see where Salvador Dalí found some inspiration. It is glorious and gory and spectacular.

Robert, being wise to these things (handy if you are the Culture editor), gives me his take. But mainly we just stand there staring at the morality play in paint in front of us, our gin-and-tonic-induced befuddlement evaporating. Then it's reverse tack. A few minutes later the concierge is shutting the trunk on our luggage and we are off to Barajas Airport.

Should you go to Madrid? Yes, even for one painting. For one deep 10-minute inhalation of culture – and a few gins the night before. You'll end up in a heavenly scene. Promise. — (M)

ABOUT THE WRITER: MONOCLE editor Tuck is also a presenter of various Monocle 24 radio programmes, including *The Urbanist*. Tune in to *monocle.com* to hear tales from the cities we love – including Madrid, of course.

Culture
—— High-brow highlights

The residents of this city know how to put on a show. In a converted butcher's shop, actors deliver quick-witted theatrical performances. You'll hear the velvety notes from a dimly lit jazz bar, which often give way to a night on the tiles when the clock strikes midnight. Then there are the masterpieces by Goya, Velázquez and Picasso that reside in galleries of impressive grandeur.

Meanwhile, more and more contemporary artists are making their mark on the city, bucking the recent economic hardships to give voice to the new kids on the block.

Madrid has perfected its cultural offerings over four centuries. Now it's time to explore the grand museums of the capital, to see a show at the Matadero, recap your Spanish film knowledge and invest in some new homegrown art.

Museums and public galleries
Artistic powerhouses

① Caixa Forum, Las Letras
Sculpted beauty

Set in a dramatically redeveloped 1899 power station in the heart of Madrid's museum district, the Caixa Forum is one of several cultural outposts bankrolled by a Catalonian finance giant. Come to visit the revolving cast of exhibitions within, which range from contemporary art to cutting-edge photography (not forgetting the substantial permanent collection).

Before dashing inside, take a moment to admire the sculptural exterior. Swiss firm Herzog & de Meuron transformed this former industrial void into an architectural spectacle: much of the base of the structure has been removed so the building appears to float, while the upper floors are coated in oxidised cast-iron, offering a new roofscape. The vertical garden – the work of French botanist Patrick Blanc – is a lush masterpiece.
Paseo del Prado 36, 28014
+ 34 913 307 300
obrasocial.lacaixa.es

On the up
—
A 24-metre-high green wall borders the square

Must-see institutions

01 Museo Nacional del Prado, Retiro: Chances are that if you're visiting Madrid you're going to brave the long lines to get your fill of Francisco Goya, Diego Velázquez and El Greco himself, Doménikos Theotokópoulos. The best way to see the royal collection of fine art – considered one of the world's best – is to book an in-house art historian to further elucidate the most significant works.
museodelprado.es

02 Museo Nacional Centre de Arte Reina Sofía, Lavapiés: The capital's modern-art museum is full of the requisite Salvador Dalí, Joan Miró and Pablo Picasso works – the latter's "Guernica" is worth the visit alone – but also includes a rare and fascinating retrospective of Civil War propaganda. Temporary exhibitions never fail to impress either.
museoreinasofia.es

② Museo ABC, Conde Duque
Drawing a crowd

Perched opposite one of the city's oldest convents in the Conde Duque district, the ABC Museum houses one of the world's most extensive collections of illustration. Built inside a converted brewery, the vast archive of around 200,000 drawings dates back to 1891, sourced from the ABC newspaper and its supplement *Blanco y Negro*.

The permanent collection provides a comprehensive look at illustrated publishing, allied to a packed programme of contemporary exhibitions that sustains a fresher forward-looking perspective.
Calle Amaniel 29, 28015
+34 917 588 379
museo.abc.es

01 **Fundación Telefónica,
Malasaña:** In one of
Madrid's first skyscrapers,
the telecommunication
giant's eponymous
four-floor foundation
explores information
as an expression of art.
And it's free.
*espacio.fundacion
telefonica.com*

02 **Fundación Mapfre,
Chueca:** Set up in 1979,
this foundation has the
self-appointed, vague
yet nonetheless noble
aim of contributing to
the wellbeing of society.
Lofty ideals aside, it still
manages to snap up some
big-name shows including
those featuring Picasso,
Jean Paul Gaultier
and Stephen Shore.
fundacionmapfre.org

③
CentroCentro, Retiro
Grand expectations

The extravagant (and costly)
reformation of the Palacio de
Cibeles into Madrid's grandiose
city hall also included a rich cultural
component. Today CentroCentro's
diverse artistic offering reflects the
city's past and present, helping to
bring the public back into the halls
of power. The focus goes beyond
art with several social spaces,
including a ground-floor press
library (media junkies take note).
Up on the third floor the newly
inaugurated Espacio-D is curated
by Ana Dominguez Siemens, who
oversees a space dedicated to
Spanish product design.

Architecture studio Arquimática
remained faithful to the original
building, utilising natural light and
casting new ideas into the grand
marble entrance hall. Don't leave
without pausing a moment on the
rooftop terrace.
*Plaza de Cibeles 1, 28014
+34 914 800 008
centrocentro.org*

*I feel like
this is
appropriate
headgear
for the
press
library*

②
Museo Sorolla, Chamberí
Art house

A visit to this gallery is a trip into
the heart of Valencian impressionist
painter Joaquín Sorolla's home,
where personal belongings are
nestled alongside masterpieces.
Built in 1911, the mansion was
converted into a museum in 1920
after the death of his widow and
time has stood still ever since. The
walls are dotted with his canvases
and each impressive work vies for
attention, especially his final,
unfinished piece. Sorolla died in
1923 and this last painting remains
on an easel alongside a collection
of paintbrushes.

The mansion's Andalusian-
styled gardens were also designed
by the painter. Punctuated by
colourful tiles, fruit trees and
waterways, the grounds are
perfect for a shady respite from
the city's heat.
*Calle General Martínez Campos 37,
28010
+34 913 101 584
museosorolla.mcu.es*

be sure to see the stables

Royal residences

01 Royal Palace, Ópera: Wander the opulent halls to discover centuries of riches accumulated by Spain's royal dynasty. Flanked by the manicured gardens of Campo del Moro and Sabatini and with 3,418 rooms, this is the biggest palace of any European capital. Don't expect to bump into any royals though: they live in a smaller palace on the city's outskirts.
patrimonionacional.es

02 Royal Palace of Aranjuez & Royal Palace of El Pardo, Aranjuez: Just a short trip beyond the city and surrounded by stunning gardens, the Royal Palace of Aranjuez and Royal Palace of El Pardo are both Unesco World Heritage listed. The former is still a functioning royal residence while the latter was once a grandiose hunting lodge that served as General Franco's official residence.
patrimonionacional.es

03 El Escorial: Following his work on the St Peter's Basilica in Rome, King Felipe II enlisted architect Juan Bautista de Toledo in 1559 to jointly design this monastery and residence in regional Madrid to secure Spain's place at the centre of the Christian world. It became a grandiloquent resting place for generations of Spanish kings instead.
monasteriodelescorial.com

Imagine how much 'vermut' you could fit in this

5

Museo Thyssen-Bornemisza, Cortes
World tour

Only this majestic 18th-century palace was fit to house Baron Thyssen-Bornemisza's extensive private collection. His museum opened in 1992 and boasts everything from Italian gothic pieces to the American hits of Edward Hopper.

The Thyssen (as it is known locally) now forms part of the city's Golden Triangle of Art, which also includes the Prado and Reina Sofia (*see page 94*). While the two bigger galleries often steal the limelight from their slightly smaller neighbour, they also attract heftier queues. Apart from delivering an in-depth tour of the world's major art movements from the 13th to 20th century, the Thyssen also includes wine-themed guided tours and a particularly well-appointed terrace restaurant.
Paseo del Prado 8, 28014
+34 902 760 511
museothyssen.org

Blank canvas
Looking to fine tune your brushstrokes? Pay a visit to the Royal Academy of Fine Arts of San Fernando. Established by royal decree in 1744, it doubles as a museum with works from the 15th to 20th centuries. Past alumni include Francisco Goya and Salvador Dalí.

6

La Casa Encendida, Lavapiés
Today's talent

If you're looking to get a gauge on the city's new artistic upstarts, this hive of multidisciplinary art is as good a starting point as any. Once home to a prominent pawnbroker, the historic building has since become a scintillating multi-level showcase of young Spanish talent.

Off the beaten track in the Lavapiés district and backed by the city's bank, La Casa Encendida (which translates to "House on Fire" – don't worry, it's a metaphor) opened in 2002. The sprawling complex includes several gallery spaces and artists' studios as well as regular workshops and interactive activities. Particular attention is given to performing arts and cinema, while a colourful rooftop terrace provides a sky-high stage for concerts featuring musical acts that frequently set the night alight.
Ronda de Valencia 2, 28012
+34 902 430 322
lacasaencendida.es

(7)

Centro Cultural de Conde Duque,
Conde Duque
Forward march

Set in the reformed 18th-century
Royal Guard barracks, this
municipal cultural complex is
now the heart of a boundless
social project that puts young
people at its forefront.

Tucked away in the university
district, the building is considered
to be one of the last examples of
classic *Madrileño* architecture;
a precursor to the Italian style that
is evident in the city's Royal Palace.
Today the rejuvenated building is
a beacon of urban renewal, housing
an assortment of exposed-brick
exhibition rooms and a red-seated
theatre, as well as rehearsal spaces
dedicated to the centre's exploration
of new performance art.

Visit in the warmer months
when a bar and open-air cinema
inject nocturnal life into two of
the three quadrangles.
Calle Conde Duque 9-11, 28015
+ 34 917 220 573
condeduquemadrid.es

Hot house
—
Matadero has helped the city's art scene blossom

Matadero Madrid
Arts centre

This former slaughterhouse in the Arganzuela district was designed by Spanish architect Luis Bellido in the early 20th century. Having been transformed by the Madrid City Council, it relaunched in 2007. It provides fertile ground for a blossoming culture scene. Director Carlota Álvarez Basso (*pictured*) co-ordinates eight institutions and a huge variety of enterprises across the 65,000 sq m venue. "It requires a lot of multitasking and good communication skills," she says. "What we try to do differently is to be more inclusive."

Since Basso took the reins in 2012 her commitment to public participation has bolstered Matadero's strong international reputation. Here we look into the venue in more detail and outline some of our favourite places.
Plaza de Legazpi 8, 28045
+34 915 177 309
mataderomadrid.org

Time to digest
—
Take a break from cultural activities at one of three food-and-drink venues at Matadero. For lunch drop by La Cantina – serving food by Chueca's restaurant Olivia te Cuida – or catch up with friends at Café Teatro. The terrace-bar of Plaza Matadero is ideal for an alfresco aperitif.

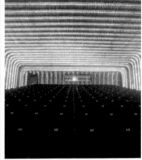

Books and reading
Literature lovers

Under the umbrella of the German Sánchez Ruipérez Foundation, which mainly focuses on readers and books, La Casa del Lector hosts exhibitions, conferences, workshops, music and film series – together with applied research – that encourage and promote reading. It's open to the public and industry professionals.

②
Visual arts
Stop and stare

Encouraging both creativity and participation, Madrid's Matadero features an exciting range of diversions. The expansive venue's numerous delights include the innovative Intermediae, which aims to prompt dialogue between artists and audiences. For accessible worldwide design stop by the Central de Diseño, a space renovated by José Antonio García Roldán.

Music
Festival vibe

Each June at the Plaza Theatre the annual Día de la Música has an eclectic line-up of must-see musicians and aspiring artists. Previous highlights include the UK's post-punk band The Horrors and Barcelona-based pop quartet Extraperlo. The stars play alongside an array of music-industry exhibitors and art displays; food and drink comes from local suppliers.

④
Film and theatre
Show time

For film head to the Cineteca, an impressive space dedicated almost exclusively to documentaries. It is also the headquarters of the Documenta Madrid film festival. Since 2003, Documenta has been welcoming around 80 international films. Meanwhile the Naves del Español, managed by the Teatro Español, is the perfect place to watch a play.

What's not to love about Julio Iglesias?

Off the wall
—
Ivorypress
is both a
publisher and
a gallery

1

Ivorypress Arts + Books, Tetuán
Hot off the press

Elena Ochoa Foster founded
Ivorypress in 1996, transforming
an old printing factory and garage
into a modern publishing house
specialising in collaborations
with artists such as Anish Kapoor,
Ron Arad and Maya Lin. It
has since evolved into a slick
multidisciplinary operation;
the retail wing has an adjacent
conference space and, since 2009,
an acclaimed gallery has also
drawn in admiring crowds.

An illustrious career has seen
Ochoa Foster curate a plethora of
prominent international exhibitions
and grace the boards of a diverse
range of museums, foundations
and international schools. The
beautifully designed space hints
at the owner's appreciation for
considered architecture: she
is married to Norman Foster.
*Calle del Comandante Zorita 46-48,
28020*
+34 914 490 961
ivorypress.com

Shedding light
—
Organised by the Association
of Galleries Arte Madrid,
Apertura takes place over
a weekend in September. It
involves 44 art galleries being
open to the public throughout
the night to celebrate the new
art season – and announce
their autumn exhibitions while
they're at it.

La New Gallery, Malasaña
Next generation

A stone's throw from the main thoroughfare of Calle Sagasta, this contemporary-art space exemplifies the wave of bold new galleries that opened in spite of the downturn. Architect Juan Valverde and lawyer Ricardo García – both avid collectors – inaugurated La New in 2012, putting on deliberately short exhibitions that range from photography to illustration, paintings, installations and video art. Their intention is to nurture homegrown artists and organise an annual art fair to further this cause.
Calle Carranza 6, 28004
+ 34 914 456 557
lanewgallery.com

❸
Galeria Helga de Alvear,
Lavapiés
Eclectic mix

Helga de Alvear's assortment of modern art is tribute to the eccentricity of a collector who has amassed one of Europe's biggest private collections; the German-born enthusiast has more than 3,000 works.

Her eye for emerging artists is key to her own commercial gallery on the Doctor Fourquet strip. And if you want to delve into her treasure trove of private acquisitions you're in luck: her Alvear's foundation opened in 2006 in the eastern city of Cáceres.
Calle del Doctor Fourquet 12, 28012
+ 34 914 680 506
helgadealvear.com

And to my left, some very pretty perches

❹
Parra-Romero, Salamanca
Family ties

Parra-Romero opened three years ago as an extension to a Madrid-based family gallery. Sat among the boutique shops of the affluent Salamanca district, Guillermo Romero-Parra took the reins of his parents' gallery in 2006 after completing a PhD at Courtauld Institute of Art in London.

Since then he has spearheaded a refocus on conceptual art and even converted a former haystack shed in Ibiza into a dynamic art space. The two spaces fuel a mutually beneficial feedback loop where creativity paves the way for artist collaborations.
Calle Claudio Coello 14, 28001
+ 34 915 762 813
parra-romero.com

❺
Travesía Cuatro, Malasaña
Back and forth

Ever since Silvia Ortiz and Inés López-Quesada flung open the shutters of their gallery in 2003, this high-spirited duo have been building a well-traversed bridge between the Spanish and Latin-American art communities. After working in Venice's Guggenheim, New York's Whitney and the Met, the pair settled back in the Spanish capital.

Having embraced emerging talent on both sides of the Atlantic, Ortiz and López-Quesada have paved a successful path that has allowed them to open a second gallery in Guadalajara, Mexico.
Calle San Mateo 16, 28004
+ 34 913 100 098
travesiacuatro.com

❻
Galeria Moisés Pérez de Albéniz,
Lavapiés
In and out

With about 20 years in the market, gallerist Moisés Pérez de Albéniz emigrated from Pamplona to Madrid when the financial crisis began to bite. Opening his gallery on the bustling Doctor Fourquet art strip was a wise move: the capital's art scene has weathered the storm and now more than 80 per cent of the trade is here.

Frequent transformations of the façade take exhibitions onto the street, while artists such as Antoni Muntadas and Dennis Adams line the walls within.
Calle del Dr Fourquet 20, 28012
+ 34 912 193 283
galeriampa.com

❼
Mondo Galería, Las Salesas
Soft power

Diego Alonso opened his small design and photography gallery on a quiet street in Madrid's Las Salesas quarter to bring the local zeitgeist to a wider audience. With this in mind he stages small seminars and holds masterclasses to encourage participation between artists and art-lovers.

While San Lucas street isn't a central artery of Madrid's beating art heart, several other galleries have sprung up in the surrounds in recent years – giving further credence to Alonso's forward-thinking forte.
Calle San Lucas 9, 28004
+ 34 913 082 325
mondogaleria.com

(8)
García Galería, Lavapiés
Future proof

Joaquín García's characteristic
bravado is as present in his daring
exhibitions as it is in his bold
predictions about the artists who
will eventually line the walls of the
neighbouring Reina Sofía Museum.
Such prescience is yet to be proven
but he has a knack for attracting
up-and-coming talent to his gallery.

"While I opened in a weak
economic climate," says García,
"tough beginnings can often turn
into stronger rewards." The space
may host small shows but the
selection gauges the breadth of
the global vanguard.
*Calle del Doctor Fourquet 8, 28012
+ 34 915 275 567
garciagaleria.com*

(9)
Machado-Muñoz, Chamberí
Complete picture

Architect and interior designer
Mafalda Muñoz joined with
photographer Gonzalo Machado
to open a gallery that makes
all the rest seem rather two-
dimensional. The focus here is
on a well-curated selection of
sculptures, contemporary furniture
and unique pieces from various
renowned artists.

Located on a quiet street, the
gallery is also used as a platform
to prompt broader conversations
about the importance of design
and architecture as a powerful art
form in its own right.
*Calle José Marañón 4, 28010
+ 34 914 120 250
machadomunoz.com*

Live venues
Show business

(1)
El Corral de la Morería, Ópera
The beat goes on

You don't need to go to Andalucía to
experience the raw, bleeding passion
of flamenco because the world's
most celebrated *tablao* is right here
in Madrid. It opened in 1956 and
owner Manuel del Rey lured talent
to the city with the promise of more
affluent audiences – before marrying
esteemed *bailaora* Blanca del Rey,
who endures as creative director.

Treating yourself to the
mouthwatering five-course
degustation menu won't just liven
your spirits: it will also ensure you
secure the best spot to marvel at
the fancy footwork.
*Calle de la Morería 17, 28005
+ 34 913 651 137
corraldelamoreria.com*

Perfect rhythm
———
Unesco declared Flamenco
an intangible part of cultural
heritage in 2010. It is joined by
two other Spanish customs:
Mallorca's Sibilia singing and
the Catalan human towers
"Castells". Madrid boasts
some of the country's best
flamenco talent, drawn by
bigger crowds.

Play time
———
Microteatro Por Dinero is up close and personal

Microteatro Por Dinero, Malasaña
Take to the stage

This peculiar outing is as oddball as it sounds: a small collection of micro-theatres located inside a redesigned butcher's where a cast of actors, directors and scriptwriters stage comfortably short immersive plays. Fifteen-minute performances are themed around different topics and small audiences literally step through the fourth wall, standing just centimetres from the feisty Spanish thespians.

Since opening as part of the Triangulo Ballesta neighbourhood renovation project, the model has been exported around Spain and from Miami to Mexico. Don't be afraid if your Spanish isn't up to scratch: performances are brief and the stories are simple, animated and hilarious. Who knows, you might even pick up a new word or two.
Calle Loreto Prado y Enrique Chicote 9, 28004
+ 34 915 218 874
microteatromadrid.es

③ Bogui Jazz, Chueca
Note form

Well-established venue Bogui Jazz has long battled against the city authorities' rigid crackdown on live music venues: it even managed to weather a painfully long city council shutdown order. But an impassioned belief in the importance of music and dance has seen the show go on: it reopened in 2005, reinvigorated and ready to reclaim its mantle as Madrid's best-loved jazz club.

Set in the lively Chueca district, it's just a short walk away from Gran Via. With an air of refined cool the club comes alive from Wednesday to Saturday. It showcases a multitude of talented homegrown jazz musicians, Latin-American songstresses and even appearances from the likes of Pedro Ruy-Blas and Freddy Cole. Just don't wake the neighbours.
Calle Barquillo 29, 28004
+ 34 915 211 568
bogui.es

La Juan Gallery, Lavapiés
Live art

The fourth wall is broken down at this gallery that presents a rather unusual – and at times provocative – form of performance art. "We swap objects for subjects, which generates a heated debate about whether this is actually art – and this is great," says Juan Gómez, a former playwright and director who runs the gallery with two colleagues. The former shop window of this once-neglected calle behind the Plaza de Tirso de Molina now captivates passers-by with a rotating streetside spectacle – and often catches many a pedestrian by surprise.
Calle Juanelo 21, 28012
+ 34 622 057 301
lajuangallery.com

Teatro La Escalera de Jacob, Lavapiés
In the spotlight

This indie-favourite performance space plays host to some of Madrid's most original shows. From magicians to stand-up comedy, the venue draws punters seeking alternative entertainment.

It's in the heart of Madrid's multicultural Lavapiés area and a seasonal terrace serves cocktails from the venue's bar, which is a coveted attraction in itself. The live shows are accompanied by a short-film festival every Tuesday, as well as workshops designed to cultivate a new generation of entertainers.
Calle Lavapiés 9, 28012
+ 34 625 721 745
teatrolaescaleradejacob.es

Is this what you mean by alternative entertainment?

Cinemas
Movie stars

Two more

01 Cines Renoir Princesa, Argüelles: Madrileños crowd into Plaza de los Cubos before watching subtitled films. The pavement outside has a Spanish walk of fame. *cinesrenoir.com*

02 Cine Ideal, Sol: The closest thing to an inner-city commercial multiplex that shows original-language films, Yelmo's Cine Ideal is next to a church. Rumour has it that Cinema 1 was built on an old graveyard. *yelmocines.es*

①
Cine Doré, Lavapiés
Old ones are the best

You may recognise the modernist façade of this quaint tangerine-coloured cinema from the Pedro Almodóvar film *Hable con ella* (*Talk To Her*). This beloved art nouveau two-screen institution was built in 1912, neatly reformed in 1923 and then, after years of resisting the advance of modern technology, had to be rescued by the ministry of culture in 1982, who turned it into Spain's official Filmotheque.

Cine Doré has had its groove back ever since, opening a shop dedicated to film in its neon-lit foyer and programming a diverse selection of favourites from the national archive. When David Lynch came to town to conduct a course on transcendental meditation, a retrospective was screened in his honour, prompting the director to sneak in to watch *The Elephant Man*, much to the audience's delight.

As you take your seat under the opulent blue ceiling of the main hall, Sala 1, don't be surprised if you're transported back to a more golden age of the silver screen. The prices – just a few euros per film – also evoke a bygone era.
Calle Santa Isabel 3, 28012
+34 913 691 125
mecd.gob.es

Madrid on film

01 Abre los Ojos (Open Your Eyes), 1997: Alejandro Amenábar's original stomps all over the (very vanilla) Tom Cruise Hollywood remake. The director managed to empty Gran Vía for one haunting scene and filmed another atop the Torre Picasso skyscraper.

02 Día de la Bestia (The Day of the Beast), 1995: A horror-themed comedy about the return of the antichrist? Only in a tempestuous city such as this could such a premise seem credible. A priest, psychic and metalhead romp from one landmark to the next in this unhinged classic.

03 The Limits of Control, 2009: Jim Jarmusch's tale follows a lone-wolf assassin across Spain on his way to kill Bill Murray. His misunderstanding with a Malasaña waiter resonates – the scene is repeated across the city ad infinitum each day.

Media round-up
Page-turners

(1)
Magazines
Paper trail

Madrid loves its magazines. Whether they cover culture like **❶** *Jot Down*, promote top illustration and graphic arts like **❷** *Minchó* and **❸** *Yokikobu* or publish essays and long-reads like **❹** *Eñe*, the focus is always on smart layouts and beautiful photography.

For the food-lovers among you, there is plenty to choose from – our favourites are food guide **❺** *Madrid Comestible* and the monthly **❻** *Tapas*, which both celebrate the best cuisine that Madrid has to offer.

And for your arts and culture intake over the weekend (and an opportunity to practice your Spanish), we suggest the **❼** *El País Semanal* supplement that comes with the Sunday edition of the Spanish daily.

(2)
Kiosco García, Retiro
Headline act

With the iconic Puerta de Alcalá gate serving as a backdrop and the Buen Retiro Park across the road, this newsstand is conveniently located and stocks a broad range of press. The multilingual selection of titles includes *The New York Times*, *El País*, *La República*, *Financial Times* and *Der Spiegel*.
Plaza de la Independencia 2, 28001
+34 914 318 819

Three more

01 Sandwich Mixto, Lavapiés: Hidden inside the Anton Martín food market, this kiosk offers a mixture of independently published books, magazines and small-run fanzines. Browse through them while enjoying a glass of *vermut* and sandwiches often served by the authors themselves.
mercadoantonmartin.com/sandwich-mixto

02 Quiosco de Bilbao, Malasaña: There are several of these ornate circular newsstands dotted around the city, marked by their pointed wrought-iron tops. This one is alongside the Bilbao Metro entrance; the curved walls open up to display an array of local and international titles, plus films and music.
Glorieta de Bilbao 7, 28004

03 Ocho y Medio Librería, Argüelles: Always a favourite with film fans, this shop sells books on cinema along with movie memorabilia. Plus there's a café, which is ideal for a pre-cinema coffee thanks to its prime location within the golden triangle of cinemas.
Calle Martín de los Heros 11, 28008

Monocle 24

When in Madrid, download our Monocle 24 radio app for fresh updates on the Spanish capital and regular check-ins from our Madrid correspondents. We also have a playlist to accompany you day and night.

Design and architecture
—— Sites for sore eyes

From the grand boulevards piercing the historic centre to the ornate fountains, arches and palaces dotting the streets, this is a city that impresses with its intentional magnificence. But wander a little longer down the narrower *calles* and you'll pick up on a different, village-like vibe, transmitted through quaint plazas, intricate balconies and ceramic-tiled façades.

As one of Europe's highest-density cities, Madrid has given rise to some creatively designed apartment buildings, from the futuristic blocks of the 1960s to a bunker-like complex originally designed for the Franco regime's military elite. A centuries-old royal legacy has also seen several private garden estates ceded back to the city in the form of vast public parks. As you traverse Madrid, colour is soaked into almost every surface, visible in the terracotta rooftops, bright buildings and painted street signs. Join us on a tour of some of the best sights the capital has to offer.

Modern architecture
Good and new

①

Palacio Longoria, Las Salesas
Whimsy and wealth

Pay no heed to the Madrid rumour mill: this is not the work of Salvador Dalí but of his fellow Barcelonés, the architect José Grases Riera. It was built for the flamboyant banker Javier González Longoria, who moved into his eponymous palace in 1904.

The Palacio Longoria is one of Madrid's modernist marvels. Grases Riera departed from the traditional style that characterises his other structures (such as the monument to King Alfonso XII that can be found in Buen Retiro Park), instead choosing to embrace more natural and whimsical motifs. The structure, not dissimilar to that of a wedding cake, stands out for its fairytale façade, while an interior dome was decorated by the esteemed stained-glass artists of La Casa Maumejean, which was founded in 1860.

It seems that the original moneyman's luck dried up early because his palace was sold to a wealthy dentist just a few years later, in 1912. Today it houses the Spanish Society of Authors and Publishers (SGAE), tasked with collecting royalties for cultural producers; unfortunately its offices are off limits to visitors.
Calle Fernando VI 4, 28004

The Palacio Longoria was the work of José Grases Riera

②
Corona de Espinas, Ciudad
Universitaria
Jewel in the crown

One of the most significant
examples of contemporary
Spanish architecture also happens
to be one of the hardest to find.
Located in Madrid's Ciudad
Universitaria district, just a short
bicycle ride from the edge of the
CBD, this functionalist structure is
infused with innovative elements
and architectural idealism.

Architects Fernando Higueras,
Antonio Miró and Rafael Moneo
joined forces to create the building,
which continues to house the
Institute of Spanish Cultural
Heritage. It was completed in 1970
and its twisted concrete forms swirl
around the main cylinder, with a
glass roof allowing the central hall's
plantlife to be drenched with rays
of natural light. A circle of concrete
spikes prompted a number of
people to dub the building the
"crown of thorns" – a name that
endures to this day.
Calle Pintor el Greco 4, 28040

Safe house
—
Corona de
Espinas was
heritage listed
in 2001

❸
Torres de Colón, Chamberí
Divided we stand

No other building polarises opinion as much as this skyscraper in Plaza de Colón. Known as "the plug-in" (the electrical as opposed to the bathroom kind) due to the two-pronged shape of its green-coloured roof, it is a building that inspires both love and hate in equal measure – but certainly never leaves onlookers lukewarm.

Antonio Lamela defied established architectural practice by building the 23-floor structure from the top down; it sprung up on the skyline when the country was slowly opening up to the outside world. Despite the Franco dictatorship at the time, modern architecture between the late 1960s and 1970s reflected a country that was still eager to make a bold international impression. The amber-coloured glass tower was originally designed for luxury apartments but became home to commercial tenants instead.
Plaza Colón, 28004

①
Casa de Campo
Wild and free

Once a gargantuan royal hunting reserve, Casa de Campo nudges the city's edge and is one of Europe's largest urban parks. A short trip on the Teleférico cable car will quickly transport you into its green depths, dropping you off on a small hill that provides a delightful vantage point of the surrounding wilderness and Madrid's white skyline off in the distance. If you're looking to escape from the urban cacophony, the tranquility of this enormous park is also only a 10-minute Metro ride from the bustling city centre.

There are plenty of other attractions hidden among the holm-oak foliage: a large rowing lake; the Madrid Zoo; and the Parque de Atracciones amusement park, providing picturesque views (assuming you're calm enough to enjoy them, of course) from high-altitude rollercoasters.
Paseo Puerta del Ángel 1, 28011

Buen Retiro Park, Retiro
Royal flush

Spain's royal legacy stretches back
to the fifth century and the vestiges
of this tradition have shaped the
capital city, particularly as palaces
and lush garden estates have been
ceded to the public.

The Buen Retiro Park was once
the domain of the royal circle but is
now the city's prized green lung.
The central lake is peppered with
rowboats; the towering fence is
circled by lithe joggers; and the
Crystal Palace, erected in 1887 to
exhibit flora and fauna from the
Philippines, is a contemporary-art
space that is one of the city's most
majestic attractions.
*Plaza de la Independencia 7, 28001
esmadrid.com/es/retiro*

Design museums

01 Museo del
Romanticismo, Malasaña:
Take a step back in time
by entering this restored
palace that pays homage
to the Romantic era. The
museum was donated to
the state in 1921 and
opened by the Marquis
of Vega-Inclán in 1924.
Today visitors can marvel
at more than 20,000 works
of art, including important
pieces by leading artists
of the time alongside
ornaments and furniture,
all spread across 26
illustrious halls.
museoromanticismo.mcu.es

02 Museo ICO, Cortes:
Tucked behind the
Spanish Parliament,
the Museo ICO initially
opened to exhibit Spain's
development bank's
modern-art collection
(including works by
Gordillo and Picasso)
but then reinvented itself
as an architecture and
urban-planning museum
in 2012. Collaborations
with prominent architects,
schools and urbanists
produce in-depth
exhibitions that encourage
visitors to question the
role of architecture as a
solution to big issues.
fundacionico.es

③
Madrid Río
Fresh impetus

The project to transform Madrid's
traffic-choked riverbank into a
10km-long park was costly but
also a game-changer for the city.
A multi-lane highway was buried in
tunnels, converting the surface into
a sprawling reserve of plant life,
bike tracks, sporting facilities and
even a small city beach (OK, it's
just concrete and sprinklers but
it's the closest thing going).

The collaborative project by
architecture studios Burgos &
Garrido, Porras La Casta, Rubio,
Álvarez-Sala and West 8 has won
several awards. *Madrileños* have also
embraced the greener banks of the
urban oasis with gusto.
Puente de Segovia, 28005

Water winner
—
Madrid Río
park skirts the
Manzanares
River

Perfectly formed
—
Madrid architects are taking on
smaller projects, showing that
interesting architecture isn't
reserved for construction on a
grand scale. A-cero has built
impressive modular homes while
Astasio y Ruiz-Rivas Arquitectos
specialises in retail interiors
such as the sleek Do Design
concept store.

①

Metropolis building, Cortes
Capital gain

This opulent triangular structure
provides a grandiose welcome to
the city's central boulevard of Gran
Vía. Insurance company La Unión
y El Fénix commissioned architects
Jules and Raymond Février to
create its new headquarters, adding
a dose of the beaux arts-style to
Madrid's skyline when it was
inaugurated in 1911.

The ornate rounded tower is
adorned with 30,000 24-carat
golden leaves. Meanwhile, the statue
of a phoenix on top is actually a
replacement: when Metropolis
Insurance purchased the building
in 1972, the previous owner's
company emblem wasn't included
in the sale and was removed. Get a
closer look from the rooftop terrace
of Hotel Principal across the road.
Calle Alcalá 39, 28014

②
Templo de Debod
Cairo calling

As the sun tips downward,
Madrid's residents gravitate to
this small park whose central
monument predates the city itself.
The Templo de Debod is an
Egyptian temple that was built
along the Nile in 2BC but then
dismantled and reassembled in
Spain in 1968 as a gesture of
friendship between the two nations.

Spain's efforts to help preserve
the Abu Simbel temples, threatened
by the construction of the Aswan
High Dam in 1960, laid the
groundwork for such a hefty gift,
which is one of the few Egyptian
monuments that can be seen
outside of the motherland.

The temple, in the Parque de
Oeste, is just a short stroll away
from Plaza España. With the trees
of Casa de Campo in the distance,
this is one of the city's best evening
vantage points to watch the sunset
as musicians tap on drums and
strum guitars.
Calle Ferraz 1, 28008

*I fancy there
are some
Egyptian
butterflies to
be had here*

③
Edificio España, Conde Duque
High value

One of Europe's first skyscrapers
was commissioned with signature
pomposity by dictator Francisco
Franco in 1953, intended as a
towering symbol of strength
and prosperity. The 25-storey
neo-Baroque-style building has
been eclipsed by more recent
skyscrapers but for many the
so-called "Spain Building" is a
weathervane of the economy.

During the peak of the
country's financial crisis the
tower stood empty: it was an
imposing and somewhat
uncomfortable reminder of the
collapsed construction sector,
illustrated by Victor Moreno's
insightful 2014 documentary
The Building. Tellingly it was
purchased in 2015 by Chinese
billionaire Wang Jianlin for a
colossal €265m. He has grand
plans to convert the monolith
into luxury apartments, a hotel
and retail hub.
Plaza de España, 28008

Lofty ambitions
———
Just across the way stands
another beacon of Franco-era
architecture: Torre de Madrid.
Designed by the Otamendi
brothers and completed in
1957, this residential and retail
complex was praised for
its metropolitan feel and is
one of the tallest buildings
in the capital.

High-density housing
Crowd pleasers

Tree-mendous
—
The Torres
Blancas are
inspired by
nature

①

Torres Blancas, Prosperidad
Singular structure

This space-age high-rise looks as
if it was lifted straight out of an
animated still of *The Jetsons*. The
cylindrical trunk lined with curved
balconies blossoms into a collection
of full-blown discs on top, creating
a comfortable platform for a
rooftop garden and pool.

Architect Francisco Javier Sáenz
de Oiza's 1969 building is revered
as one of the best examples of
extreme Spanish organicism, taking
cues from the world of nature and
trees. The elliptical forms adorning
the interior and exterior capture
the bold symbolism of that period.

Yet the name, White Towers, is
misleading on two counts. First,
it was initially envisioned as a
gleaming beacon of white marble
but dust mixed with the cement,
resulting in an undeniably brown
colour instead. Second, there were
plans for a further two towers but
financial restraints resulted in just
one; plural in name but not nature.
Avenida de América 37, 28028

I know a
dog called
Franco.
No, wait...
Fido

②

Edificio Princesa, Conde Duque
Distinctively democratic

Iconoclastic architect Fernando
Higueras designed this brutalist
complex for the Spanish military
housing agency in the twilight
years of the Franco dictatorship.
Inaugurated in 1975, the modern
structure starkly contrasts with the
traditional regime that many of its
residents once swore to defend.

Formerly dominated by Franco's
cadre, in recent years the Edificio
Princesa has been disrupted by the
inevitable march of change as a
generation of spirited young
Spaniards have snapped up
properties. Located on the
uppermost corner of the Conde
Duque district, Higueras's vision
of functional, high-density
architecture has withstood the test
of time and is one to be celebrated.
This vine-draped, bunker-like
building is a concrete testament to
the contradictions and optimism of
Spain's transition to democracy.
Calle Alberto Aguilera 1, 28015
edificioprincesa.com

**Transport hubs
and buildings**
On the move

②
Atocha Station, Atocha
Pet project

Spain has one of the best rail systems in Europe and all tracks lead to Atocha Station in the epicentre. A major fire damaged the original 1851 structure, prompting the city to enlist Alberto de Palacio y Elissague (who also designed Retiro Park's Palacio de Cristal) and French *magicien du fer* Gustave Eiffel (you may have heard of his tower in Paris) for the 1892 rebuild.

The hollowed-out, inverted hull is made of wrought iron and glass, covering a 4,000 sq m space with an indoor rainforest and one big pond full of red-eared slider turtles – a consequence of Spaniards offloading unwanted pets.

Plaza del Emperador Carlos V, 28045

①

Viaducto de Segovia, Ópera
Arc of history

Eugenio Barrón first constructed a towering bridge of iron and wood in 1874 to link the Royal Palace and the Basílica de San Francisco el Grande Church. It has undergone several rebuilds and been mired in controversy ever since.

Damage during the Civil War prompted authorities to recast the bridge with reinforced cement in 1942; it was restored again in 1977 and 1978, leading to several accidental deaths. In 1998 a transparent barrier was erected to prevent others falling from the high edge. Despite its grim foundation, the rationalist structure has been the backdrop for many Spanish films.

Calle Bailén, 28010

117

③
Adolfo Suárez Madrid-Barajas
Airport, Barajas
Height of good taste

Constructed in 1927, Spain's
largest airport became one of
Europe's busiest hubs following an
impressive expansion by Antonio
Lamela and Richard Rogers, who
completed Terminal 4 in 2006.

Renamed after the late Spanish
prime minister who led Spain
through the patchy sky of its
democratic transition, the Adolfo
Suárez Madrid-Barajas Airport is
characterised by a long wooden
arciform ceiling that is held up
by brightly coloured columns that
capture the city's chromatic palette.
Avenida de la Hispanidad, 28042
+34 913 211 000
aeropuertomadrid-barajas.com

Making waves
—
An undulating
ceiling unrolls
at the airport

❶
Coloured buildings
Kaleidoscopic city

Madrid's street-side colour palette
is suitably cheerful and any stroll
through Malasaña, Las Letras or
Lavapiés will be tinged with bright
reds, imperial blues, saffron yellows
and pastel-coloured paint.

Science suggests that the colour
scheme of our cities shapes our
daily mood but in Madrid, a city
notorious for its sunny disposition,
the question of chromatics boils
down to a classic chicken-or-egg
dichotomy. Do the high spirits
stem from the brightly coloured
surroundings or do *Madrileños*
choose to paint their buildings
with pigments that reflect their
pre-existing vivacity? It's a vivid
citywide debate.

②
Stone animals on buildings
Creature creations

The city's coat of arms features
a bear climbing a *madroño*
(strawberry tree); Calle Alcalá's old
Palacio de la Equitativa is dotted
with de-tusked elephant heads; and
a clutch of other creatures adorn
the city's modernist marvels. The
incorporation of animals into
architecture is a recurring motif.

However, these creatures were
not all born of the same litter. A row
of penguins sprang up on the roof
of the old Cervezas de Santander
brewery on Calle Fernando VI as
part of the building's rebrand, while
just across the intersection the
lizards decorating Benito González
del Valle's 1911 residence earned it
the nickname of La Casa de los
Lagartos (House of Lizards).

While Barcelona has more
modernist edifices than Madrid, a
few architects still went against the
grain of the Spanish capital's more
traditional vernacular. Their legacy
is an array of animals that continues
to embellish the concrete jungle.

Fatima-hand door knockers
Artistic appendages

Vestiges of the Islamic caliphate are
dotted across the Iberian Peninsula
despite a document by Holy
Roman Emperor Charles V that
banned Islamic symbols in 1526.
The enduring show of hands can
be seen on doors across the city
(and Spain), remnants of an era
when the Moors ruled the land and
placed the hand of Fatima on their
front doors to ward off evil spirits.

While the significance of these
historic hand-me-downs is lost on
many, the door knockers are joined
by other Islamic relics such as the
squared towers of old mosques
(now converted Catholic churches)
and the geometric forms inscribed
on ancient tiles.

Tío Pepe

Tío Pepe is more than just a
piece of branding; this neon-lit
sherry advertisement is an icon.
Erected in 1936, it survived the
Civil War, Franco's dictatorship
and a request by Apple to have
it removed from its flagship
store's roof. It has earned its
place in the city's heart of
Puerta del Sol.

④

Wrought-iron balconies
Windows of opportunity

A ubiquitous (yet often overlooked) part of the city's vernacular, ornate cast-iron railings cover most large windows in the city centre. The shallow balconies stretch all the way back to the Mudejars of the 12th century and well into the 19th century on façades such as the Hotel Atlántico on Gran Vía.

However, they also speak to the character of the capital's residents. Apartments in the historic centre are often poky and their inhabitants are invariably a social lot. As such, these wrought-iron railings are perfect for providing the necessary vantage point to survey the street, chat to (and, where necessary, spy on) neighbours or simply breathe in the night air.

It's an unfortunate truth that as smoke-guzzling traffic has swamped the city, nosey neighbours of old have been relegated indoors – but they can still be spotted peering through the curtains.

Excuse me, this wrought-iron lamp is taken

❺

Illustrated street signs
Out on the tiles

Madrid is crisscrossed by a raft of eccentrically named streets, many of which are accompanied by urban legends that have been thoroughly cemented into the cityscape. Calle de la Cabeza (Head Street) was inspired by the gruesome story of a servant who one day decapitated his cruel master; Calle del Desengaño (Disappointment Street) tells the dubious tale of a deceptive lady ghost; and Calle de San Cosme y San Damián pays homage to twin brothers who performed a miraculous leg transplant in the third century (or so the legend has it).

In 1991, the city council teamed up with ceramic-tile artist Alfredo Ruiz de Luna to illustrate these sometimes far-fetched, occasionally macabre but proudly told origin stories on more than 500 street signs, etching them permanently into the city's collective memory. Keep an eye out.

Sport and fitness
── Health kicks

Good weather, well-manicured parks, a newly redeveloped riverside area and a plethora of polished sporting facilities: this active city has plenty to offer residents who want to burn off some steam.

Work out in well-equipped fitness centres, jog past various iconic monuments with our four suggested running routes or head to one of several pools for a few laps, soaking up some sunshine while you're at it. If you're looking to shake up your standard fitness regime we've included a few tips on where to ski, golf, play football and stretch to your heart's content. There are also some handy hints on where to smarten up before you head out for a relaxing evening post exercise.

① Metropolitan Abascal Gym, Chamberí
Award-winning heavyweight

A short jog from the historic centre, this Spanish chain pulls out all the stops for its flagship gym in the Chamberí district. A pantheon of health and fitness, it claimed the Madrid city council's award for commercial architecture.

A spacious main floor is furnished with enough machinery to satisfy the needs of the most demanding fitness buffs, and a team of instructors and masseurs is on hand to offer assistance. The big draw is the in-house spa, which features a large hydro-massage pool, Jacuzzi and Turkish baths. A second, slightly smaller location in the Palacio Santa Ana offers a similar experience.
Calle José Abascal 46, 28003
+34 914 514 466
clubmetropolitan.net

② Gymage Lounge Resort, Malasaña
Beacon of style

When a group of young entrepreneurs from Valencia came to town with a bold plan to transform a dilapidated cinema, locals were sceptical. Nonetheless, it didn't take them long to convert the entire building into a health and hospitality complex that has blossomed into a powerful magnet for bronzed bodies – often found striking a toned pose at the rooftop bar and restaurant.

Style and flair coalesce to create what can only be described as a Valencian enclave in the heart of the Spanish capital. The theatre and restaurant on the ground floor are complemented by a well-stocked health food shop, a busy gym occupies the middle level and up on the rooftop a small "solarium" pool is prime real estate when Madrid's summer temperatures soar.
Calle de la Luna 2, 28004
+34 915 320 974
gymage.es

⓷
Open-air gym, Buen Retiro Park
Alfresco all-rounder

Under the watchful gaze of Lucifer
himself, the Buen Retiro Park's
open-air gym attracts legions of
fitness freaks from sunrise to sunset.
Set alongside one of the world's only
public monument to the fallen angel,
this extensive collection of bars and
beams speaks to the city's love of the
outdoors and healthy lifestyle.

Regular users include the joggers
circling the park's perimeter, yoga
and martial arts classes on the
surrounding lawns and a street
workout team whose members, apart
from flexing their muscles on the
bars, are usually close by to provide
a helping hand.
*Puerta del Ángel Caído, Calle
de Alfonso XII, 28014*

Swimming pools
Dive in

Ⓘ
Centro Deportivo Municipal
Escuelas de San Antón, Chueca
Inner sanctum

For those not content with merely
clocking up the lengths this modern,
25-metre municipal pool offers great
views over central Madrid. Right in
the heart of Chueca, the upper-
level pool is the star attraction of
a leisure centre built in collaboration
with a nearby school and Madrid's
college of architects.

This is one of the few indoor
swimming options in the city centre
(most pools favour the outdoors)
and there is also a daily schedule
of fitness classes, as well as a sauna,
steam room and Turkish baths.
*Calle de la Farmacia 13, 28004
+34 918 289 006
cdmescuelassananton.com*

Hotel Emperador rooftop pool,
Ópera
Warm welcome

The scorching heat can sometimes
be too much to bear in the city
centre but it all depends on your

perspective. Head up to the
10th floor of the historic Hotel
Emperador and any heat-induced
duress will quickly fade away.

From the comfort of your
deckchair, lap up sweeping views
of the Royal Palace and Gran Vía
as you temper the heat with regular
dips in the pool. From 14.30, €45
gets you unlimited access to the
rooftop terrace and pool, plus
a sizeable three-course lunch.
*Gran Vía 53, 28013
+34 915 472 800
emperadorhotel.com/madrid*

⓷
Piscina Municipal El Lago, Casa de
Campo
Beach substitute

Escape the summer heat with a trip
to the edge of Casa de Campo's
green expanses: a short ride on the
number 10 Metro will transport you
to this impressive outdoor complex
with two swimming pools.

Popular among beach-deprived
Madrileños, the facilities are
interspersed with small cedar forests
and gardens full of people reclining
between dips. In true Spanish form,
the municipal café sells beer and *tinto
de verano*. In the hotter months it gets
very busy from mid-afternoon so
stake out your spot before lunch.
*Paseo Puerta del Ángel 7, 28011
+34 914 630 050
madrid.es*

Grooming and haircare

01 Malayerba, Malasaña:
The team at this traditional
barber in Malasaña's famed
Plaza Dos de Mayo have
created their own range of
organic hair products.
barberiamalayerba.es

02 Peluqueros Urbano,
Malasaña: These
boisterous barbers add
their unique *barrio* touch
to the inner-city Malasaña
district. Brothers Miguel
Ángel and José Luís took
over from their father in
2007, continuing a legacy
of haircutting that started
in 1907.
+34 915 329 126

03 Corta Cabeza, citywide:
The quirkiness of Luciano
Cañete and Luis María
Rodriguez's hairdressing
experience is the closest
thing you will get to a
live-action Almodóvar
film. The flamboyant
team of scissor-wielding
professionals has fuelled
the shop's success, with
two extra salons having
opened in the city.
cortacabeza.com

04 Salon44, Malasaña: Xavi
García's long hairdressing
and fashion career is
channelled into this sleek
salon, beauty-treatment
centre and shop. Besides
a line of hair products,
customers can buy
García's own fragrance,
which was created in
collaboration with Madrid
perfumery Oliver&Co.
salon44.es

05 Maison Eduardo
Sánchez, citywide:
Colombian-born Eduardo
Sánchez opened two
unisex hair studios in
2014 after 25 years in the
industry. He is supported by
a multilingual team of hair
and beauty professionals.
*maisoneduardosanchez.
com*

Alternatives
Sporting heroes

I'm sure I'll
get the call
from Real
Madrid any
day now

① Football, Madrid Río
Get your kicks

The Spanish are passionate
about football; resistance to their
infectious enthusiasm is futile.
If you are looking to burn some
real calories, go the whole nine
yards and sign up for a game
at one of many lively municipal
pitches around the city.

In particular, lace up your boots
and head down to the facilities
on the regenerated banks of the
Manzanares River. Put the ball in
the back of the net and you will
earn the respect of fellow *futbolistas*
as well as creating the opportunity
to have *cañas* (small beers) after
the game – it's a key element of the
sporting tradition.
Paseo Chopera 10, 28045

② Skiing, Sierra de Madrid
Onward and downward

At 667 metres above sea level,
Madrid is Europe's highest-altitude
capital (unless you want to get
pernickety and count Andorra),
and with the Sierra de Guadarrama
mountain range towering on the
horizon, you may be wondering
where the nearest Spanish ski
lodge is.

Fortunately, it's not too far.
About 60km from the city centre,
Puerto de Navacerrada offers 10km
of pistes. Taking the Cotos pass
will bring you to a second resort,
Valdesquí, which has 26 slopes. It's
an easy two-hour train journey to
Puerto de Navacerrada Station.
*puertonavacerrada.com;
valdesqui.es*

Going for gold
———
Despite the city's unsuccessful
Olympic bids – see our essay
on page 84 – 'Madrileños'
shine on domestic and
international sporting fronts.
Fernando Martín Espina in
particular was a legend; he
competed in multiple sports
and was the first Spaniard to
break into the NBA.

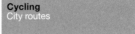

Flagged up
—
The practice facilities are second to none

①

Madrid Rio
Urban adventure

STARTING POINT: Matadero Cultural Precinct
DISTANCE: Only 4km – but you can continue along the river if you like

Inaugurated in 2011, the Madrid Rio regeneration project has reclaimed the riverbanks with a 10km-long verdant park and leisure complex. Start at Matadero, the former slaughterhouse and livestock market turned arts centre; you can hire a bike at Mobeo inside. Then turn down the winding paths to your right. Along the way you'll speed past the Playa de Madrid, Madrid's answer to an urban beach, and the gleaming metallic spirals of Arganzuela Bridge, before you pass under the beautifully restored Segovia Bridge.

Take the ramp on your far right and cross to the opposite bank. If you're there in the evening you'll be treated to a spectacle from the base of the Toledo Bridge: the white Royal Palace and Almudena Chapel burn bright orange and pink just before the sun dips down.

③

Golf Canal, Chamberí
Above par

The first bricks of this extensive sporting facility were laid in 1930 by a group of sporty workers who banded together to make use of a vast inner-city space atop a subterranean reservoir. What began as a simple municipal football field and swimming pool has greatly expanded over the years and has been joined by Golf Canal: a modern complex that includes some of the city's best *padel* courts (one of Spain's most played sports), and two football fields. For golfers there is a nine-hole course, driving range and putting school.
Avenida Filipinas s/n, 28003
+34 915 357 614
golfcanal.com

MadYoga, Malasaña
Holistic haven

Gonzalo Retenaga transformed a former fashion showroom into this inner-city yoga venue, made up of three different studios. He runs the space with dancer Alicia Chico and yoga teacher Borja Sainz, with the intention to marry ancient yogi traditions and philosophy to the 21st-century lifestyles of their clientele.

It is open six days a week and found on one of the quieter streets of Malasaña. The lithe team of instructors covers a breadth of styles, with classes from those suitable for beginners to challenging workshops for the experienced.
Calle Pizarro 19, 28004
+34 915 315 011
madyoga.es

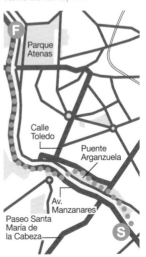

Parque Atenas

Calle Toledo

Puente Arganzuela

Av. Manzanares

Paseo Santa María de la Cabeza

Ⓕ

Ⓢ

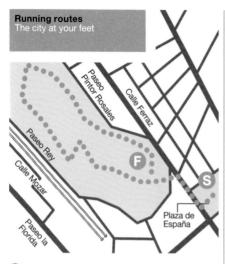

Running routes
The city at your feet

①

Parque Oeste
Sunset run

DISTANCE: 2km
GRADIENT: Flat, with a decline and a few stairs to climb
DIFFICULTY: Easy
HIGHLIGHT: Perched right on the city's edge, your starting point is an Egyptian temple
BEST TIME: Early morning or at sunset
NEAREST METRO: Plaza de España

Start at the base of Plaza de España. Cross the road and follow the curved pedestrian path to the right until you reach a steep flight of stairs set into the hillside. Bounce up the steps to the top, where you'll be greeted by an Egyptian temple: the Templo de Debod. Built on the Nile in 4BC, it was brought to Spain in the 1960s.

Run parallel to the main road until you reach the vine-draped Horno de Asar, an abandoned restaurant. On the right a path descends into the heart of the park. Run towards the building in the far distance; this is the launching point for the famed Teleférico cable car. Resist the urge to jump aboard, instead veering left and continuing down onto the road. Turn left again, where you'll find a long, flat stretch of secluded road, which mainly serves residential traffic. It is straddled by a large rose garden on the left and sweeping views onto Casa de Campo in the distance on the right. Your cue to turn left is the unmistakable iron-hued hull of the Príncipe Pío train station just ahead on your right. Before you reach the station, turn left and spring up the widely spaced steps.

At the top, head towards the small car park and up the palm-tree adorned flight of stairs, which will bring you back to the illuminated Templo de Debod. This is also one of Madrid's best vantage points to watch the sunset, so take a few moments to catch your breath and stretch on the grass on either side of the temple.

②

Buen Retiro Park
Lap of the gods

DISTANCE: 4km
GRADIENT: Mostly flat with one testing incline
DIFFICULTY: Hard
HIGHLIGHT: Running through the middle of the picturesque park is worth the lap alone and the open-air gym is a muscle-toning bonus
BEST TIME: Any time of day
NEAREST METRO: Atocha (note: not Atocha Renfe)

Starting on the corner of Cuesta de Moyano and Paseo de Prado, you'll hardly be in the zone for perusing literature but as you make your way up the incline of Cuesta de Moyano, take a few moments to admire the community of vintage booksellers with quaint wooden stalls shaded by parasols. Once you get to the top, cross the roundabout and enter through the Buen Retiro Park's dual Ángel Caído ("Fallen Angel") gate.

This is where the tough part begins: you'll need to power up the hill – a good 200 metres – until it plateaus. You'll be able to see the Fallen Angel statue at the end of the road – one of the world's only known monuments to Lucifer. Once you reach it, continue in the same direction and just before you reach the main paved perpendicular road, turn left up the Paseo de Julio Romero de Torres heading towards the Palacio de Cristal off to your left. Soldier on up the path, running between two mini-towers, and up to the artificial lake. Take a wide berth around it, behind the half crescent of columns that form the Alfonso XII monument and past the Casa de Vacas (Cow House) cultural centre, and turn left when you reach the perimeter fence.

When you arrive at the main gate you can either head across the road for a protein-rich breakfast at Harina or continue running along the perimeter until you return to the gate of the Fallen Angel.

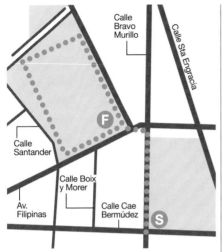

③

Parque Santander
Friendly all-weather track

DISTANCE: 1.3km
GRADIENT: Flat
DIFFICULTY: Easy
HIGHLIGHT: The only easy-to-access rubber-surfaced
    running track in the inner city
BEST TIME: Evening: although this is a popular time
    of day, there's a contagious social atmosphere
    on the track
NEAREST METRO: Canal

The Santander Park in Canal is where to find the
perfect carefree running track on which to crank up
the volume on your iPod and not have to worry about
the threat of traffic.

Inaugurated in 2007 as part of a €50m upgrade
of the Golf Canal sporting complex (*see page 125*)
the rubber-sealed route – which is wide enough for two
or three runners – is 1.2km long with blue marker
posts every 100 metres. It is at the top of the Chamberi
district so catch the Metro to the Canal Station (just six
stops from Metro Sol on Line 2).

As you exit the station, run up Calle Bravo
Murillo, turn left at the intersection and cross the road
to enter the complex. Once inside the perimeter fence,
take to the track and join other dedicated runners as
they circle football and *padel* fields, as well as a driving
range. Don't worry about the latter: the nets are high
enough to protect you from any wayward golf balls.

Once you're done you can head to the stretching
facility a few metres from the track's edge. However,
if you are here during the late evening you may have
to improvise on the surrounding park benches as
the place is busiest just before Spanish dinner time
(21.00). It also proves to be particularly popular on
Sunday mornings.

④

Paseo de la Castellana
Architectural tour

DISTANCE: 3.5km
GRADIENT: Mainly flat
DIFFICULTY: Easy
HIGHLIGHT: Central location and lined with
    architectural icons
BEST TIME: Early morning or late evening to avoid
    the traffic
NEAREST METRO: Gregorio Marañon

Start at the Gregorio Marañon Metro and head south
down the central path on the right-hand-side traffic
island. Continue until you reach Plaza Colón. Cross the
road to your right and wait at the pedestrian crossing
in front of amber-glassed skyscraper Torres de Colón,
named after Christopher Columbus.

You're now on the section called Recoletos. To your
left sits the Spanish National Library, while on your right
is the tiled, gazebo-like Café El Espejo terrace. Pass by
the Cibeles fountain, marvelling at the magnificence of
the Cibeles Palace as you hook right and past the ancient
fountains and statues until the Fountain of Neptune,
where you should skirt around the left-hand edge of
the roundabout until the Prado Museum. To avoid the
dawdling tourists, cross back onto the island running
down the middle of the Paseo de Prado (same road,
different name) and ending when the paved path does, or
continue along the path until you can see Atocha Station.

• •
Where to buy
———

For a good pair of running shoes go to the Nike
shop on Gran Vía (*nike.com*). Or, if you prefer,
check out the trainers and accessories in Duke
(Conde Duque 18, 28015).
• •

Walks
—— Find your own Madrid

Don't worry: you're not the first person to be confounded by Madrid's complicated network of narrow streets. But getting lost is all part of the adventure, right? For those of you looking to lap up the local flavour without mislaying your sense of direction along the way, we've concocted five themed routes through the city's most vibrant *barrios*. They are all jam-packed with our favourite haunts and home-cooked treasures.

NEIGHBOURHOOD 01

Malasaña and Conde Duque
Colourful creative hub

If you're looking for action, the Malasaña district offers it in spades. The brightly coloured streets are lined with a patchwork of bars, restaurants, specialist shops, galleries and design studios, while homes are inhabited by Madrid's lively young creatives. Losing oneself among the labyrinthine lanes will lead to plenty of pleasant surprises but the best way to sample the energy is a tour of the closely connected plazas. Filled with characters young and old, these vibrant community hubs are brimming with noise and activity. Wander a little further and the surrounding streets will reveal why this neighbourhood provides such fertile ground for intrepid entrepreneurs, rookie retailers and tasty restaurants.

The city's comfortable climate and social spirit mean that Malasaña's plazas pulsate with life from sunrise to sundown. But why stop there? In recent years the adjoining Conde Duque district has benefitted from its neighbour's overflow of creative enterprise. Crossing Calle San Bernardo will take you into the depths of this inner-city enclave that, while slightly more refined, has retained a distinctly local flavour. Take your time; any semblance of a rush and you'll stick out like a sore thumb. Set aside a long afternoon, pull up a chair, sip on copious *copas* and people-watch well into the night.

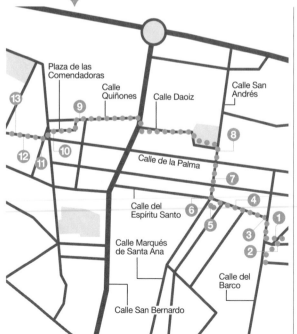

March of gentrification
Malasaña and Conde Duque walk

Waiting patiently in front of the San Ildefonso Church you'll find a stoic fixture of the community known locally as "*la niña*". One of four statues of women dotted around the neighbourhood, from her vantage point she's seen Plaza San Ildefonso slowly transform into the loud beating heart of Malasaña.

Until 1970 the plaza was occupied by an enclosed street

Getting there
———
Running approximately every 10 minutes, the M2 bus services the Malasaña area from both the Sevilla and Argüelles districts. Alternatively, Tribunal Station on Metro Lines 1 and 10 is a five-minute walk, as is Chueca Station on Line 5.

market but today terrace seating takes centre stage. Pull up a chair at ❶ *Naïf* for a snack or beer, or duck into espresso bar ❷ *Bianchi Kiosco Caffè* for a take-away coffee to perk you up.

Exit the plaza via Calle Corredera Alta de San Pablo and carry on until you reach the corner canteen known as ❸ *Greek & Shop*. The combined restaurant and retail venture is a feast of fresh and packaged Hellenic gastronomy. Turn left down Calle Espíritu Santo (Holy Spirit Street) passing eyewear shop ❹ *Óptica Caribou*, which sells its own brand alongside international frames. If it's still before 21.00 you might even catch the old fishmonger displaying his glistening seafood in a defiant stand against the tide of gentrification.

A few more paces will take you to Plaza Juan Pujol, named after a journalist and double agent from Murcia. Either feast on *raciones* of traditional Spanish food – including Madrid's famous calamari sandwich – at ❺ *El Balcón de Malasaña* or pull up a green chair on the terrace of eccentric restaurant ❻ *Ojalá*. There's also a semi-secret stairway providing a convenient getaway option.

Continuing down Calle San Andrés, look out for the old pharmaceutical ads for toothache remedies and "inoffensive smokeables" on the tiled façade of the Laboratorio Juanse. Directly opposite, an old ice factory has been converted into ❼ *La Industrial*, a thriving co-working centre for start-ups.

A few more metres down the slope the classically styled bar

❽ *Pepe Botella* is a relaxed spot for a glass of Spanish Rueda wine.

Named after the 1808 uprising against the French, the adjacent Plaza Dos de Mayo is filled with students from the nearby music school strumming their guitars alongside happy packs of energetic dogs. After soaking up the atmosphere, exit via Calle Daoiz, cross Calle San Bernardo and go up Calle Quiñones, where the Tolkienesque tower of the Church of Montserrat stands tall above what was once a women's prison. A short walk along the narrow paved street leads to Plaza Comendadoras. Enjoy a drink at the art deco corner of ❾ *Café Moderno* or a refreshing iced coffee across the plaza at ❿ *Federal Café*.

Continue down the pedestrian Calle Cristo and either stop at ⓫ *La Canela*, where you'll be rewarded with a free book with every drink, or continue until you spot the small, eccentric, black-humoured jewellery shop ⓬ *Taller de Feeas*. End with a sweet *vermut* at the historic ⓭ *La Taberna de Corps* – you've certainly earned it.

NEIGHBOURHOOD 02
Lavapiés
Exotic mosaic

The multicultural make-up of Lavapiés has defined this district for centuries. It was originally the thriving Jewish quarter until the Alhambra Decree expelled all Jews from Spain in 1492. Many years later it still attracts diverse diasporas, from Africa to India and Asia. The result is a rich mosaic of exotic food, fashion and cultural fun.

A swirl of myths and theories surround the origin of the neighbourhood's name. Some say Lavapiés – which literally translates to "wash feet" – has religious connotations derived from an ancient custom where the devout would wash their feet in a central fountain before entering the temple. Others believe it stems from the more practical custom of washing off the perennial dust in the small streams that once flowed down into the main plaza.

Both the fountain and streams have since vanished but the neighbourhood that has sprung up in their wake has been shaped by a conspicuously international flavour: more than half of the residents in Lavapiés were born overseas. Whether you're sampling the spices of Indian and Bangladeshi cuisine on Calle Lavapiés, yielding to the anarchic tunes inside an African jazz club or savouring the revival of the San Fernando food market, this zigzag tour is a vibrant, noisy and spice-laden feast.

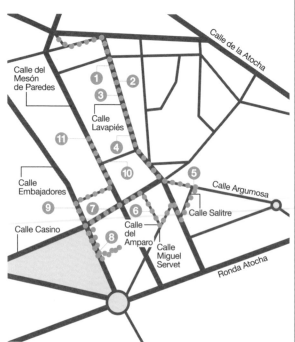

Magical mystery tour
Lavapiés walk

Start among the flower stalls of Plaza Tirso de Molina, heading downhill via Calle Lavapiés. As you cross Calle de la Cabeza (Head Street) look up for the illustrated street sign retelling the macabre tale of a servant who decapitated his master. A few steps away is a small bookshop and gastro bar called **1** *El Dinosaurio Todavía Estaba Allí* combines literary adventure with a daring menu (try the venison ragout), exemplifying how Madrid bookshops have been reinventing themselves to stay afloat.

Continue down the street until the beautifully tiled corner façade of **2** *La Escalera de Jacob*. This small bar is also a well-known theatre; the "cave" below hosts late-night performances, monologues and hilarious improv and is open until late. Across the small plaza the corner restaurant **3** *Mano a Mano* is overseen by affable owners who offer a range of Spanish rice dishes (it's not all paella, you know) and Spanish delicacies such as *navajas* (razor clams).

As you continue downhill you will pass a small multi-tiered neighbourhood plaza, nicely appointed with colour by artist Cristina Gayarre's bright mural. As the street opens up, the friendly yet persistent touts of this south-Asian strip will try to lure you into their Indian and Bangladeshi restaurants. **4** *Shapla* is certainly worth a visit but they're all equally delicious. As you reach the bottom of the slope, cross the Lavapiés

Address book

01 El Dinosaurio Todavía
   Estaba Allí
   Calle Lavapiés 8, 28012
   +34 910 826 270
   eldinosaurio.es
02 La Escalera de Jacob
   Calle Lavapiés 9, 28012
   +34 625 721 745
   *teatrolaescaleradejacob.
   com*
03 Mano a Mano
   Calle Lavapiés 16, 28012
   +34 914 687 042
   restaurantemanoamano.es
04 Shapla
   Calle Lavapiés 42, 28012
   +34 915 281 599
   *shaplaindianrestaurant.
   com*
05 La Playa de Lavapiés
   Calle Argumosa 9, 28012
   +34 911 429 603
   laplayadelavapies.com
06 Los Chuchis
   Calle del Amparo 82,
   28012
   +34 911 276 606
07 Gau&Café
   Calle Tribulete 14, 28012
   +34 915 282 594
   gaucafe.com
08 La Tabacalera
   Calle Embajadores 53,
   28012
   latabacalera.net
09 San Fernando Market
   Calle Embajadores 41,
   28012
   +34 915 272 512
   mercadodesanfernando.es
10 A Love Supreme
   Calle Caravaca 17, 28012
   *alovesupremelavapies.
   com*
11 Baobab
   Calle de los Cabestreros 1,
   28012

Plaza veering to the left of the Valle-Inclán National Centre for Dramatic Arts to soak up the relaxed cheer of Calle Argumosa. There's a seemingly endless selection of bars and restaurants stretching all the way down to the Reina Sofia Museum but take a rest in ❺ *La Playa de Lavapiés*, which has a playful beachside theme including a beach salad and the Popeye crêpe.

Crossing the street, follow Calle Salitre, cross Calle Valencia and turn left down Calle Miguel Servet. Peak inside one of the city's proudly preserved *farmacias* on your immediate left; a prominent chandelier still hangs from this one's ceiling above the medicine. Turn right at Calle Amparo, where homely restaurant ❻ *Los Chuchis* is headed by a pair of Englishmen proudly serving British cuisine to (often sceptical) Spaniards, proving just how far Lavapiés' gastronomic offering extends.

Turn left onto Calle Tribulete and walk past the halal butchers and Bangladeshi barbers until you reach the modern Uned building.

Don't be fooled by the sturdy metal doors: head inside through the deserted foyer and take the lift up to one of the city's largest rooftop bars and restaurants, ❼ *Gau&Café*.

Once you come back down, follow the street to Calle Embajadores. Turn left and you'll reach tobacco factory turned bohemian cultural centre ❽ *La Tabacalera*, while a right turn leads to the ❾ *San Fernando Market*, whose glowing revival has been spearheaded by entrepreneurs.

Cross the adjacent Plaza Agustín Lara going up Calle del Mesón de Paredes, where jazz club and restaurant ❿ *A Love Supreme* combines tasty African food with free-spirited live music. A short stroll uphill will take you to the terrace of Senegalese restaurant ⓫ *Baobab*, where you can end with a well-proportioned meal as you survey the sights and sounds of Plaza Nelson Mandela, recently renamed after local residents gathered here to pay tribute following the death of the former South African president.

Getting there

If the weather is in your favour, Plaza Tirso de Molina is a pleasant 20-minute walk from all neighbouring 'barrios'. Alternatively, Tirso de Molina Station on Metro Line 1 is located right on the square, as is the bus stop for routes M1 and 65.

NEIGHBOURHOOD 03

Chamberí
Plaza living

Just to the north of Malasaña's bohemian buzz and west of the establishment stronghold of Salamanca lies the characterful *barrio* of Chamberí. Coming to life as Madrid expanded beyond its city walls during the 19th century, Chamberí housed workers from the industrial sector as well as a burgeoning middle class, becoming home to the likes of impressionist painter Joaquín Sorolla, writer Benito Pérez Galdós and poet Antonio Machado. Today, amid its attractive tree-lined streets, you'll find mid-rise residential buildings with ornate balconies alongside a blend of stately embassies, wedding-cake churches and the remnants of Chamberí's industrial origins.

It remains a bastion for Madrid's wealthier set, yet its central location and proximity to the city's university gives it a younger vibe too. Characterised by a lack of pretension, Chamberí is packed with restaurants, bars, bookshops and galleries that, coupled with an urban design that centres on the beautiful Plaza de Olavide, make it eminently walkable and full of life.

A glut of recent restaurant and bar openings have added gravitas to its reputation as one of Madrid's finest tapas districts. We recommend taking a gastronomic walk through Chamberí to investigate further. Timed best during late afternoon, this will give you the perfect flavour of quotidian *Madrileño* life.

Gastronomic amble
Chamberí walk

Stepping out of ❶ *Quevedo Metro station* brings you onto the bustling Glorieta de Quevedo, named after the Spanish golden-age writer. From here head south down the boutique-lined Calle Fuencarral before turning left onto Calle Olid, where a short walk will take you to one of Madrid's little-known gems.

The circular Plaza Olavide forms a natural break in the regular network of streets carving up Chamberí and, fittingly, provides its residents with a space to escape from their daily routine. A central fountain and children's play area are ringed with trees and the sound of flamenco is never far away. The sought-after outdoor tables are seen as a barometer for Madrid's seasons, with the re-emergence after winter of scarf-clad *Chamberileros* dictating when spring has truly arrived.

Among the many characterful establishments circling the plaza is ❷ *Arco Iris*. Neon-lit and full of kitsch Spanish memorabilia, its continued popularity is assured by the cool beer and excellent tortilla it serves. The latter – a time-honoured recipe of eggs and potato dished up to share between two or four people – is reason enough to stop. For a lighter bite, ❸ *Mama Campo* on the other side of the

Getting there

It's easy to get to Chamberí from most parts of Madrid. Take Metro Line 2 to Quevedo Metro Station, which deposits you in the heart of the district. Alternatively, find a BiciMad bike to pedal your way to Glorieta de Quevedo, which has several docking stations along its side streets.

Address book

plaza is a more recent addition but its organic food and eco-wines have made it a firm favourite.

Refreshed and reinvigorated, head north up Calle Murillo and turn left onto Calle Quesada, followed by a right onto Calle Eloy Gonzalo. Even on this busy main road you'll see terraces overrunning the street as you make your way up towards the Iglesia Metro. On your left you'll see the ❹ *Parroquia de Santa Teresa y Santa Isabel*, which with its twin spires makes a stunning statement among Chamberí's largely residential architecture. At this point the chance exists to detour five minutes down Paseo General Martínez Campos to Museo Sorolla, the beautiful home of impressionist painter Joaquin Sorolla. Yet for those with a taste for tapas, we recommend taking a left at Iglesia onto Calle Santa Engracia until you reach the base of Calle Ponzano on the opposite side of the road.

The legend goes that Calle Ponzano is one of Europe's most restaurant-adorned streets. The only question is where to start. We like ❺ *Muta*: with a name meaning "change" or "mutate", and with themes ranging from Balearic to Brazilian, its light bites and beer selection are worthy of exploration. Over the road, drop into ❻ *López Carnes y Fiambres*, a shop that makes an art of charcuterie, with garlic, meat and artichokes taking the place of high fashion in boutique-grade window displays.

Further up on the left you'll find the acclaimed ❼ *Sala de Despiece*, where fresh fish is dished up (from menus penned daily by hand) amid polystyrene cartons and a cool crowd. Continue along Ponzano

and you'll find the beer-hall ambience of ❽ *La Factoria de Ponzano*, a new opening with an industrial-chic aesthetic, generous servings of *empanadas* and *croquetas* and Galician beer on tap.

Still hungry? Keep walking and you'll arrive at ❾ *Noama*, a tapas bar with character far outsizing its small footprint; while ❿ *Cervecería El Doble*, easily identified by its striking azulejo tiling, is a great spot for a *caña*. For those still seeking gastronomic satisfaction, walk further up Calle Ponzano past the kids' patchwork classes and monastery and you enter the fiefdom of Argentine chef Estanislao Carenzo, the brains behind both the pizza joint ⓫ *Picsa* and ⓬ *Sudestada*, which offers Asian-Argentine fusion cuisine.

NEIGHBOURHOOD 04
Barrio de Las Letras
Creative vibe

Madrid's illustrious Barrio de Las Letras is a charming old-town area and the historic Plaza de Santa Ana is one of its main draws. The *barrio* is named in honour of the literary legends who lived here during the *Siglo de Oro* (the golden age of Spanish literature) between the 15th and 17th centuries and the neighbourhood's eastern boundary is defined by Paseo del Prado up to the Thyssen-Bornemisza Museum.

Pay your respects at the door of Miguel de Cervantes, author of *Don Quixote*, who lived at Calle Cervantes 2. A small plaque marks the space where his house once stood. He was buried at the nearby Convento de las Trinitarias. Today the convent is closed to the public but an annual mass is held on 23 April to mark the anniversary of his death. The house of another great wordsmith, Lope de Vega, is now a museum that celebrates Spain's most prolific playwright's life and work.

Las Letras has had a recent facelift but has held on to its bohemian vibe and aura of history and tradition. Today the area is sprinkled with art galleries, antique-furniture shops and plenty of street art, and is slowly garnering a reputation as Madrid's design district. As you meander along the paved streets of this arty *barrio*, there are plenty of *tabernas* to ensure you're well fed. Start your walk bright and early to enjoy the neighbourhood at its best.

Under the influence
Barrio de Las Letras

Start your day at the lively Plaza Santa Ana, where the beautiful **❶** *ME Madrid Reina Victoria Hotel* dominates the square. The rooftop terrace offers spectacular views of Madrid but if you are in a hurry to start your walk, grab a coffee to-go at the bar on the ground floor. Across the square is **❷** *Teatro Español*; the grand neoclassical building dates back to the late 1800s.

From there take Calle del Príncipe until you reach Calle de Las Huertas, make a sharp left and at number 20 you will see **❸** *Amieva-México*. Pop in for a selection of antique maps and engravings from around the world. Continue walking on Las Huertas and be sure to look down: you will see engraved quotes on the pavement from the works of celebrated Spanish authors such as Miguel de Cervantes, Lope de Vega and Pedro Calderón de la Barca.

Make a left on Calle León and you'll pass by **❹** *Farmacia León*. Even if you are not in need of any medicine or cosmetics, this pharmacy is worth a visit: the façade is covered in beautiful blue-and-white tiles and elaborate illustrations.

Across the street from Farmacia León is **❺** *Brown Bear Bakery*. This is the place to head for artisanal breads and pastries. Opt for an almond croissant or a stack of thick pancakes covered in maple syrup. After a sugary treat, continue walking along Calle León. There are plenty of cute clothes shops to keep you occupied. One not to miss is **❻** *Pipoca*, which sells womenswear by Spanish designers. When done shopping, keep walking down Calle

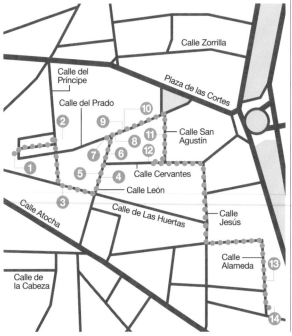

León until you reach Calle del Prado and on the corner you will find ❼ *Lamucca*. The restaurant has five branches in Madrid but the one in Las Letras is probably the most popular among those who prefer a casual lunch. It is open every day from 13.00 till late and offers hearty dishes at good prices in a fuss-free environment.

On the opposite corner is ❽ *Vincci Soho Hotel*. It's impossible to miss thanks to the beaming lizard installation on the façade. Continue up Calle del Prado and at number 21 you'll find ❾ *Ateneo de Madrid*. The iconic cultural institution was designed in 1884 by architects Enrique Fort and Luis Landecho. Adorned with Greek Revival paintings by Arturo Mélida, today it hosts exhibitions and plays.

Next door is ❿ *One Shot Prado 23*, an arty hotel that, besides its modern interiors, features a rotating roster of works by young artists. From there continue on Calle del Prado until you reach Plaza de las Cortes and then turn right onto Calle San Agustín. At number 4 you will find interior design shop ⓫ *Lou*

& Hernandez, which is a treasure trove of vintage mirrors, Nordic furniture and home decorations from all over Spain.

When you reach Calle Cervantes take a right; at number 11 is the ⓬ *Casa Museo Lope de Vega* where you can get to know the life and times of Spain's most famous playwright. Next walk back along Calle Cervantes until you arrive at Calle Jesús. Turn right and continue your walk via Calle Moratín until you see Calle Alameda; turn right there and after one block you'll be at ⓭ *La Fábrica* at number 9. Whether you are after a design book, a bottle of wine or a piece of local art, this publisher, gallery and shop is the perfect one-stop destination. Rest your legs and rehydrate at the bar.

If eager for more cultural encounters, continue further down until you see the striking ⓮ *CaixaForum Madrid*. Housed in an old power station, the museum opened in 2007. It was designed by Swiss architects Herzog & de Meuron, while the imposing green wall on the neighbouring building is courtesy of botanist Patrick Blanc.

Getting there

The best way to get to Barrio de Las Letras is to head to Sol station on Metro Lines 1, 2 or 3, which is a five-minute walk away heading south along Calle Espoz y Mina.
To arrive right on Plaza Santa Ana, take the M1 bus travelling from Embajadores.

Address book

01 ME Madrid Reina Victoria Hotel
Plaza Santa Ana 14, 28012
+34 917 016 000
melia.com

02 Teatro Español
Calle del Príncipe 25, 28012
+34 913 601 480
teatroespanol.es

03 Amieva-México
Calle de Las Huertas 20, 28012
+34 914 299 476

04 Farmacia León
Calle León 13, 28014
+34 914 295 158

05 Brown Bear Bakery
Calle León 10, 28014
+34 913 690 587
brownbearbakery.es

06 Pipoca
Calle León 5, 28014
+34 608 492 872

07 Lamucca
Calle del Prado 16, 28014
+34 915 210 000
lamuccacompany.com

08 Vincci Soho Hotel
Calle del Prado 18, 28014
+34 911 414 100
vinccihoteles.com

09 Ateneo de Madrid
Calle del Prado 21, 28014
+34 914 296 251
ateneodemadrid.com

10 One Shot Prado 23
Calle del Prado 23, 28014
+34 914 204 001
hoteloneshotprado23.com

11 Lou & Hernandez
San Agustín 4, 28014
+34 914 202 750
louyhernandez.com

12 Casa Museo Lope de Vega
Calle Cervantes 11, 28014
+34 914 299 216
casamuseolopedevega.org

13 La Fábrica
Calle Alameda 9, 28014
+34 912 985 523
lafabrica.com

14 CaixaForum Madrid
Paseo del Prado 36, 28014
+34 913 307 300
obrasocial.lacaixa.es

NEIGHBOURHOOD 05
Chueca and Las Salesas
Vital revival

Chueca was a rather neglected neighbourhood until about two decades ago, when Madrid's LGBT community adopted the troubled *barrio* and transformed it into a gleaming garrison of bars, lively cafés and independent boutiques. In recent years the northern part, known as Las Salesas (between Calle Sagasta and Plaza de Chueca), has established itself as an affluent retail and arts hub, while Chueca is the nucleus of Orgullo Gay Madrid, one of the biggest LGBT festivals in the world. It is held in the first week of July.

The area's gradual transformation and gentrification can be seen in the redevelopment of some of its iconic buildings, such as Mercado San Antón. The food market reopened in 2011 after a major refurbishment and has retained its meat and fish stalls as well as now housing an art gallery, well-stocked bar and rooftop terrace.

The neighbourhood really comes alive every evening with plenty of bars and clubs that stay open well into the small hours. Among the best known are Delirio, Truco, Fulanita de Tal, Why Not? and Long Play. Start your neighbourhood walk around lunchtime to get to know Chueca's more sober side, when cafés are serving freshly brewed coffee and the doors of the city's most diverse shops are still open.

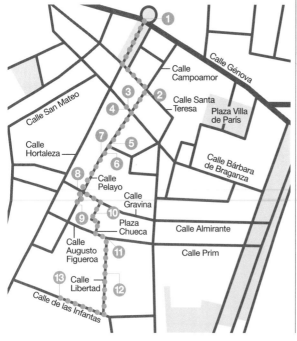

Free spirit
Chueca and Las Salesas walk

Start your walk at ❶ *Metro Alonso Martínez* on Plaza Santa Bárbara and turn left onto Calle Santa Teresa. At number 8 you'll find ❷ *Olivia Te Cuida*, one of the best-kept secrets on the food scene. It is the perfect pitstop for a tasty breakfast or hearty lunch. This intimate café opens at 09.00 and its homemade dishes are served till 18.00.

Once sated head down Calle Pelayo, one of the main retail streets in Las Salesas – but just before you start exploring all the shops, turn right onto Calle Fernando VI. At number 9 you'll see the flower-filled façade of ❸ *Margarita Se Llama Mi Amor*. This florist with two neighbouring shops offers lavish flower arrangements and same-day deliveries. In addition it sells potted plants and vases and will prepare special arrangements for events. If this splendour is not enough, across the street is the flamboyant ❹ *Palacio Longoria*. The extraordinary building was designed in 1902 by José Grasés Riera as a residence for banker Javier González Longoria. Today it's home to the Spanish writers' and artists' association (Sociedad General de Autores y Editores) and is known as the SGAE building.

Continue walking down Calle Pelayo until you reach the inviting shopfront of ❺ *Espacio Brut*. Besides its in-house line of furniture, this interior-design shop offers a smart selection of modern and vintage pieces by the likes of Arne Jacobson and Alfredo Häberli. Just a few steps away is ❻ *Oleoteca Chueca la Chinato*, which specialises in virgin olive oil. Also on offer is

a selection of treats such as baby squid, mussels, lobster pâté and gourmet chocolates.

Next on your shopping spree is ⓭ *Guille García-Hoz's showroom*. The designer offers lovely home accessories such as porcelain tableware, wallpaper, candles and glassware. If thirsty, take a right onto Calle Gravina; at number 3 is ⑧ *Frutal*, where you can enjoy a freshly squeezed juice named after one of Madrid's districts. We suggest you opt for the "Chueca", of course; it's a punchy mix of lemons and oranges.

After this quick refreshment head back to Calle Pelayo. Just a few more steps on your left is ⑨ *Cube Peluquerías*. This hair salon has a few locations in the city and is known for its quick, fuss-free cuts (walk-ins are welcome).

Turn right onto Calle Gravina and cross the lively ⑩ *Plaza de Chueca* and then go down Calle Barbieri until you reach ⑪ *Mercado San Antón*. The younger and less flashy sibling of Mercado San Miguel opened in 2011 after an extensive renovation. The must-

Getting there

One of the best-connected hubs on Madrid's Metro network, Alonso Martínez Station is serviced by Lines 4, 5 and 10, from which you can easily stroll into Chueca. Chueca Station on Line 5 sits right in the heart of the 'barrio'. To remain above ground, hop on a BiciMad bike.

see market offers a mix of stalls and seating for tapas and drinks. Among its vendors are La Imperial with its signature Andalusian-style calamari and La Casa del Bacalao, known for its cod tapas; Puturrú de Foie serves an affordable assortment of Basque *pintxos*. Head to the top-floor terrace for a quick vermouth and then to ⑫ *Taberna La Carmencita* on Calle Libertad. This cosy establishment serves the best traditional dishes in the area. The Spanish omelette and the paella are a must, plus there is a great selection of Spanish wines. Reservations are recommended.

Finally, wrap up the day with an alfresco drink on the roof of ⑬ *Room Mate Óscar Hotel*, which offers great views of Plaza Vázquez de Mella. Óscar is one of the four Room Mate hotels in Madrid. This outpost in Chueca is the liveliest and the most fun, given its proximity to all the clubs in the area. The terrace reopened in 2015 after being spruced up by interior designer Tomás Alía. There are Balinese beds beside the pool and an extensive bar offering 30 bespoke cocktails. *Salud!*

Address book

01 Metro Alonso Martínez
    Plaza de Santa Bárbara,
    28004
02 Olivia Te Cuida
    Calle Santa Teresa 8,
    28004
    +34 917 020 066
    oliviatecuida.blogspot.com
03 Margarita Se Llama
    Mi Amor
    Calle Fernando VI 9, 28004
    +34 910 259 809
    *margaritasellamamiamor.
    wordpress.com*
04 Palacio Longoria
    Calle Fernando VI 4, 28004
    +34 913 499 550
    sgae.es
05 Espacio Brut
    Calle Pelayo 68, 28004
    +34 910 258 963
    espaciobrut.com
06 Oleoteca Chueca la
    Chinata
    Calle Pelayo 62, 28004
    +34 911 526 599
    lachinata.es
07 Guille García-Hoz's
    showroom
    Calle Pelayo 43, 28004
    +34 910 224 745
    guillegarciahoz.com
08 Frutal
    Calle Gravina 3, 28004
    +34 649 061 800
    frutal.info
09 Cube Peluquerías
    Calle Pelayo 28, 28004
    +34 915 226 129
    *cubepeluquerias.wix.com/
    cube2015*
10 Plaza de Chueca
    28004
11 Mercado San Antón
    Calle Augusto
    Figueroa 24, 28004
    +34 913 300 730
    mercadosananton.com
12 Taberna La Carmencita
    Calle Libertad 16, 28004
    +34 915 310 911
    tabernalacarmencita.es
13 Room Mate Óscar Hotel
    Plaza de Vázquez de
    Mella 12, 28004
    +34 917 011 173
    oscar.room-matehotels.com

Resources
—— Inside knowledge

So far you've learnt how to order a nice *vermut* or where to get the juiciest *bocadillo de calamares*. We've also shown you Madrid's best galleries and our favourite examples of the capital's architecture, old and new.

On these pages you'll find some handy local expressions, discover which events you really should check out while in town (depending on when you visit), get tips on how to navigate your way through the city's picturesque *calles* and learn which tunes we think make the perfect soundtrack for doing so.

Transport
Get around town

01 **Madrid Metro:** The city is best discovered by foot but scorching summer temperatures will often force you below ground. The Madrid Metro is a world-class, easy-to-use and cheap underground system. Buy a 10-trip Metro ticket: it's much easier than trying to use the complicated ticket machines.
metromadrid.es

02 **Cercanías:** You'll need a separate ticket but the Cercanías train network traverses the metropolitan area in just over 10 minutes. It's the quickest option to the airport's Terminal 4 and there's even a station in Puerta del Sol, the city's centre.
renfe.com

03 **BiciMad bike scheme:** People said a city bicycle scheme wouldn't work but municipal authorities smartly opted for electric bikes to help with those steep inclines. Visitors can jump on a bike for €2 an hour, which can be paid by card.
bicimad.com

04 **On foot:** The narrow streets of the city centre lend themselves to a relaxed walking tour. This is the best way to discover Madrid's seemingly endless offer of bars, restaurants and shops, and to soak up the city's contagious atmosphere.

05 **AVE high-speed train:** Spain has one of the world's most extensive high-speed rail networks and the capital's central location means the coast is only ever a two- to three-hour train ride away.
renfe.com

06 **Private car hire:** Taxis in Madrid offer affordable, fuss-free service to and from the airport but if you need a private driver your best bet is Aero City.
+34 917 477 570
aerocity.com/en

Vocabulary
Local lingo

So your Spanish isn't up to scratch? Belt out a few of these words and you'll impress your *Madrileño* hosts with your effortless (albeit basic) command of the language.

01 **Anda ya!:** you're kidding!
02 **Buenas:** generic all-day greeting
03 **Caña:** small beer
04 **Copa:** alcoholic drink
05 **Mazo:** a lot/loads
06 **Mola!:** cool!
07 **Perdona:** excuse me
08 **Qué tal?:** how are you?
09 **Un gato:** a cat – also a third-generation-plus *Madrileño*
10 **Una movida:** a serious problem

Soundtrack to the city
Five top tunes

01 **Joan Manuel Serrat, 'Mediterraneo':** A Catalan singing about the Mediterranean? Yes, but this classic tune is Spain's real national anthem.

02 **Fangoria, 'A quien le importa':** The group's singer, neo-goth-pop queen Alaska, is famous throughout the Spanish-speaking world and this 2010 hit added new sparkle to her crown.

03 **Michael Fassbender, 'I Love You All':** Even though this gem from the film *Frank* is about an obscure bar, Fassbender hits the nail on the head, singing, "El Madrid it's nice to see you..." Crank this one up as you disembark.

04 **Manu Chao, 'Merry Blues':** From the album *Próxima Estación: Esperanza*, this track samples the announcement on the Madrid Metro.

05 **Mecano, 'Hoy no me puedo levantar':** The signature tune of Madrid's 1980's glam-pop outfit lives on – it was even the title of a stage musical about the group on Gran Vía.

Best events
What to see

01 Madrid Fusión & Gastrofestival: Unsurprisingly, Spain's most renowned fairs are food-related festivals. *January, madridfusion.net; gastrofestivalmadrid.com*

02 ArcoMadrid: Spain's premiere contemporary-art fair. *February*

03 Mercedes-Benz Fashion Week: Held biannually. There has been a bigger focus on nurturing up-and-coming designers in recent years. *February & September, mbfashionweek.com*

04 Semana Santa: Haunting Easter processions spill out of churches to the sound of drums and trumpets. *Easter week, semanasantamadrid.es*

05 San Isidro festival: Madrid's patron saint gives the city yet another reason to party – and slip into traditional dress. *15 May*

06 La Feria del Libro: A fortnight-long celebration of reading that turns the Buen Retiro Park into a literary hub. *May-June, ferialibromadrid.com*

07 DecorAccion: An interior-decorating event that transforms the entire Las Letras district each June. *June, decoraccion.nuevo-estilo.es*

08 Orgullo Gay: Madrid's gay pride isn't a sideline event: the whole city comes out to party in what has been billed as the annual summer catharsis. *July, madridorgullo.com*

09 Trashumancia festival: Shepherds and their flocks of sheep invade the city once a year to promote grazing and sheep-migration rights. *October/November*

10 San Silvestre Vallecana New Year's Eve Marathon: Madrid's oldest road race attracts 40,000 people for a 10km evening run – before eating 12 grapes at the stroke of midnight on 31 December.

Rainy days
Weather-proof activities

It may not pour down that often, but the city's altitude means winter temperatures can get quite cold. If the day turns overcast, here are a few ideas for some extra cheer.

01 Lose yourself in the Prado or Reina Sofía: The Museo Nacional del Prado is dauntingly big but it boasts some of history's most significant works of art (*see page 94*). We recommend requesting a private guided tour with a friendly art historian. You could easily spend the other half of the day at the Reina Sofía, Spain's premiere modern-art museum – start by having lunch at its Jean Nouvel-designed restaurant. *museodelprado.es; museoreinasofia.es*

02 Food-market walk: After years of public and private investment, the city's network of gastronomic markets is one of its best assets. Many combine retail with spectacle in an effort to attract the hungry crowds but the real attraction is the well-cooked food. Check out our two-page spread on the city's best markets from page 46.

03 Take the high-speed train to Toledo or Segovia: So the weather's miserable in the city centre? Check the forecast in the historic towns of Toledo or Segovia – you may have better luck. The historical capital before the Moorish conquest, Toledo is only a 33-minute train ride away from the elegant 19th-century Atocha Station (worth seeing in any case for its well-preserved beauty). You can be in Segovia in about 25 minutes via the high-speed AVE (from Chamartín Station). The picturesque town is known for its monumental Roman aqueduct, built around 50 AD but continuously in use well into the 20th century.

Sunny days
The great outdoors

As you're in one of Europe's sunniest capitals, chances are you're going to get a healthy dose of vitamin D. Here are three hot tips on where to soak up the sun.

01 Rooftop terraces: The lack of a beach means *Madrileños* have sought out more creative ways to spend their blazing summer days. An increasing number of sky-high oases have been popping up across the city, providing inner-city sanctuaries from the scorched concrete below. Many include well-stocked bars, delicious restaurants and, in some cases, even a refreshing pool. See page 45 for our top picks and remember: these *azoteas* are also the best places for a night-time tipple.

02 Visit a Madrid winery by Metro: A short 30-minute journey by Metro to Arganda del Rey will deliver you within walking distance of one of Madrid's main wine-producing regions. We recommend Madrid Wine Routes for one of several historically themed bilingual tours just outside the city, ranging from revisiting the arrival of the Roman empire over two millennia ago to following in the footsteps of Spain's Bourbon royal house. *madridrutasdelvino.es*

03 Wander the La Latina labyrinth for tapas and treasure: La Latina is at its most alive every Sunday for the El Rastro flea market. Thousands of people congregate in the surrounding streets for tapas and drinks, savouring the weekend until its dying breath – but you can enjoy the colour and taste of this vibrant district on any day of the week. We recommend wandering down the El Rastro strip and into the side streets to visit colourful bric-a-brac and antiques dealers.

About Monocle
—— Step inside

In 2007, Monocle was launched as a monthly magazine briefing on global affairs, business, culture, design and much more. We believed there was a globally minded audience of readers who were hungry for opportunities and experiences beyond their national borders.

Today Monocle is a complete media brand with print, audio and online elements – not to mention our expanding retail network and online business. Besides our London HQ we have seven international bureaux in New York, Toronto, Istanbul, Singapore, Tokyo, Zürich and Hong Kong. We continue to grow and flourish and at our core is the simple belief that there will always be a place for a print brand that is committed to telling fresh stories and sending photographers on assignments. It's also a case of knowing that our success is all down to the readers, advertisers and collaborators who have supported us along the way.

In the know
—
Madrid correspondent
Liam Aldous

1
International bureaux
Boots on the ground

As well as our HQ in London and seven international bureaux, we also rely on first-hand reporting from our contributors in more than 35 cities around the world. Among them is Madrid correspondent Liam Aldous, who's been with MONOCLE since 2011 and is also a regular on Monocle 24 discussing everything from politics to literature and art. For this travel guide he worked with a team of writers in the city to ensure we have covered the best food, retail, hospitality and entertainment the city has to offer. The aim is to make you, the reader, feel like a local when you visit.

On *air*
——
Our radio studios are on site at Midori House

2
Radio
Sound approach

Monocle 24 is our round-the-clock radio station that was launched in 2011. It delivers global news and shows covering foreign affairs, urbanism, business, culture, food and drink, design and print media. When you find yourself in Madrid you can listen to *The Globalist*, our morning news programme that is the perfect way to start the day in Europe; Monocle 24's editors, presenters and guests set the agenda in international news and business. We also have a playlist to accompany you day and night, regularly assisted by live sessions that are hosted at our Midori House headquarters.

3
Print
Committed to the page

MONOCLE is published 10 times a year. We have stayed loyal to our belief in quality print with two new seasonal publications: THE FORECAST, packed with key insights into the year ahead, and THE ESCAPIST, our summer travel-minded magazine. To sign up visit *monocle.com/subscribe*. Since 2013 we have also been publishing books, like this one, in partnership with Gestalten.

4
Online
Digital delivery

We also have a dynamic website: *monocle.com*. As well as being the place to hear Monocle 24, we use the site to present our films, which are beautifully shot and edited by our in-house team and provide a fresh perspective on our stories. Check out the films celebrating the cities that make up our Travel Guide Series before you explore the rest of the site.

5
Retail and cafés
Good taste

Via our shops in Hong Kong, Toronto, New York, Tokyo, London and Singapore we sell products that cater to our readers' tastes and are produced in collaboration with brands we believe in. We also have cafés in Tokyo and London serving coffee and Japanese delicacies among other things – and we are set to expand this arm of our business.

Join us

There are lots of ways to be part of the ever-expanding MONOCLE world whether in print, online, or on your radio. We'd love to have you join the club.

01
Read the magazine

You can buy MONOCLE magazine at newsstands in more than 60 countries around the world, or get yourself an annual subscription at *monocle.com*.

02
Listen to Monocle 24

You can tune in to Monocle 24 radio live via our free app, at *monocle.com* or on any internet-enabled radio. Or download our shows from iTunes or SoundCloud to keep informed as you travel the globe.

03
Subscribe to the Monocle Minute

Sign up today to the Monocle Minute, our free daily news and views email, at *monocle.com*. Our website is also where you'll find a world of free films, our online shop and updates about everything that we are up to.

MONOCLE – keeping an eye and an ear on the world

Monocle

EDITOR IN CHIEF & CHAIRMAN
Tyler Brûlé
EDITOR
Andrew Tuck
SERIES EDITOR
Joe Pickard

**The Monocle Travel Guide
Series: Madrid**
GUIDE EDITOR
Liam Aldous

DESIGNER
Jay Yeo

PHOTO EDITORS
Ana Cuba
Poppy Shibamoto

PRODUCTION
Jacqueline Deacon
Dan Poole
Sonia Zhuravlyova
Chloë Ashby

Writers
Mikaela Aitken
Liam Aldous
María Arranz
Pablo Bautista
David Bernal
Nelly Gocheva
Marcus Hurst
Pablo León
Jason Li
Luis Mendoza
Paula Móvil
Ben Olsen
Chiara Rimella
Marie-Sophie Schwarzer
Rodrigo Taramona
Ben Taylor
Andrew Tuck

Chief photographer
Gianfranco Tripodo

Still life
David Sykes

Photographers
Víctor Garrido
Mariano Herrera
Salva López
James Rajotte
Ben Roberts

Illustrators
Satoshi Hashimoto
Tokuma
Hans Woody

Research
Mikaela Aitken
Lucy Atkinson
Joey Edwards
Kurt Lin
Tim Lucraft
Chiara Rimella
Marie-Sophie Schwarzer
Matthew Singerman
Ben Taylor
Taymour Williams

Special thanks
Julie Alpine-Crabtree
Emma Chiu
Paul Fairclough
Chris Hughes
Tim Lucraft
Julia Newcomb
Andrew Urwin

The collection

We hope you have found the Monocle Travel Guide to Madrid useful, inspiring and entertaining. There's plenty more to get your teeth into: our London, New York, Tokyo, Hong Kong, Bangkok, Miami, Istanbul and Rio de Janeiro guides are already on the shelves, with Paris, Singapore, Vienna, Honolulu and Sydney joining them in the coming months.

O1
London
The sights, sounds and style of the British capital.

O2
New York
We get a taste for the best of the Big Apple.

O3
Tokyo
Japan's capital in all its energetic, enigmatic glory.

O4
Hong Kong
Get down to business in this dramatic city.

O5
Madrid
A captivating city abuzz with spirit and adventure.

O6
Bangkok
Stimulate your senses with the exotic and eclectic.

O7
Istanbul
Where Asia and Europe meet – with thrilling results.

O8
Miami
We unpack the Magic City's box of tricks.

O9
Rio de Janeiro
An enchanting city of beaches and bossa nova.

IO
Paris
Walk this way through the City of Light.

Buy today at all good bookshops

Or visit the online stores at:
monocle.com
shop.gestalten.com